D0956104

DISCARD

Abortion

Other Books in the History of Issues series:

THE
HISTORY
OF
ISSUES

Abortion

Jacquelyn Landis, Book Editor

GREENHAVEN PRESS

An imprint of Thomson Gale, a part of The Thomson Corporation

THOMSON

™

GALE

Detroit • New York • San Francisco • San Diego • New Haven, Conn.
Waterville, Maine • London • Munich

Bonnie Szumski, *Publisher*
Helen Cothran, *Managing Editor*

© 2006 Thomson Gale, a part of The Thomson Corporation

Thomson and Star Logo are trademarks and Gale and Greenhaven Press are registered trademarks used herein under license.

For more information, contact:
Greenhaven Press
27500 Drake Rd.
Farmington Hills, MI 48331-3535
Or you can visit our Internet site at http://www.gale.com

ALL RIGHTS RESERVED
No part of this work covered by the copyright hereon may be reproduced or used in any form or by any means—graphic, electronic, or mechanical, including photocopying, recording, taping, Web distribution, or information storage retrieval systems—without the written permission of the publisher.

Articles in Greenhaven Press anthologies are often edited for length to meet page requirements. In addition, original titles of these works are changed to clearly present the main thesis and to explicitly indicate the author's opinion. Every effort is made to ensure that Greenhaven Press accurately reflects the original intent of the authors. Every effort has been made to trace the owners of copyrighted material.

Cover photograph reproduced by permission of © Micah Walter/Reuters/CORBIS.

LIBRARY OF CONGRESS CATALOGING-IN-PUBLICATION DATA

Abortion / Jacquelyn Landis, book editor
    p. cm. -- (The history of issues)
    Includes bibliographical references and index.
    0-7377-1903-6 (alk. paper)
    1. Abortion. 2. Abortion--Law and legislation. 3. Abortion--Social aspects. I.
Landis, Jacquelyn. II. Series.
    HQ767.A1533 2006
    363.46--dc22

                                                                    2006041176

Printed in the United States of America
10 9 8 7 6 5 4 3 2 1

Contents

Chapter One: Rights and Constitutionality

SHATFORD LIBRARY

NOV   2007

1570 E. Colorado Blvd.
Pasadena, CA 91106

Henry Hyde's 1976 amendment banned Medicaid funding for abortions, which made abortion increasingly inaccessible for poor women.

Chapter Two: Morality and Abortion

Pro-life activists turned to violence when peaceful methods to stop abortion failed. Arson was a favored tactic, but activists resorted to kidnapping as well.

Chapter 4: Should Abortion Rights Be Restricted?

Medical professionals have a duty to provide reproductive services such as abortion even if they are personally opposed to them.

Foreword

In the 1940s, at the height of the Holocaust, Jews struggled to create a nation of their own in Palestine, a region of the Middle East that at the time was controlled by Britain. The British had placed limits on Jewish immigration to Palestine, hampering efforts to provide refuge to Jews fleeing the Holocaust. In response to this and other British policies, an underground Jewish resistance group called Irgun began carrying out terrorist attacks against British targets in Palestine, including immigration, intelligence, and police offices. Most famously, the group bombed the King David Hotel in Jerusalem, the site of a British military headquarters. Although the British were warned well in advance of the attack, they failed to evacuate the building. As a result, ninety-one people were killed (including fifteen Jews) and forty-five were injured.

Early in the twentieth century, Ireland, which had long been under British rule, was split into two countries. The south, populated mostly by Catholics, eventually achieved independence and became the Republic of Ireland. Northern Ireland, mostly Protestant, remained under British control. Catholics in both the north and south opposed British control of the north, and the Irish Republican Army (IRA) sought unification of Ireland as an independent nation. In 1969, the IRA split into two factions. A new radical wing, the Provisional IRA, was created and soon undertook numerous terrorist bombings and killings throughout Northern Ireland, the Republic of Ireland, and even in England. One of its most notorious attacks was the 1974 bombing of a Birmingham, England, bar that killed nineteen people.

In the mid-1990s, an Islamic terrorist group called al Qaeda began carrying out terrorist attacks against American targets overseas. In communications to the media, the organization listed several complaints against the United States. It generally opposed all U.S. involvement and presence in the Middle East. It particularly objected to the presence of U.S. troops in Saudi Arabia, which is the home of several Islamic holy sites. And it strongly condemned the United States for supporting the nation of Israel, which it claimed was an oppressor of Muslims. In 1998 al Qaeda's leaders issued a fatwa (a religious legal statement) calling for Muslims to kill Americans. Al Qaeda acted on this order many times—most memorably on September 11, 2001, when it attacked the World Trade Center and the Pentagon, killing nearly three thousand people.

These three groups—Irgun, the Provisional IRA, and al Qaeda—have achieved varied results. Irgun's terror campaign contributed to Britain's decision to pull out of Palestine and to support the creation of Israel in 1948. The Provisional IRA's tactics kept pressure on the British, but they also alienated many would-be supporters of independence for Northern Ireland. Al Qaeda's attacks provoked a strong U.S. military response but did not lessen America's involvement in the Middle East nor weaken its support of Israel. Despite these different results, the means and goals of these groups were similar. Although they emerged in different parts of the world during different eras and in support of different causes, all three had one thing in common: They all used clandestine violence to undermine a government they deemed oppressive or illegitimate.

The destruction of oppressive governments is not the only goal of terrorism. For example, terror is also used to minimize dissent in totalitarian regimes and to promote extreme ideologies. However, throughout history the motivations of terrorists have been remarkably similar, proving the old adage that "the more things change, the more they remain the same." Arguments for and against terrorism thus boil down to the same set of universal arguments regardless of the age: Some argue that terrorism is justified to change (or, in the case of state terror, to maintain) the prevailing political order; others respond that terrorism is inhumane and unacceptable under any circumstances. These basic views transcend time and place.

Similar fundamental arguments apply to other controversial social issues. For instance, arguments over the death penalty have always featured competing views of justice. Scholars cite biblical texts to claim that a person who takes a life must forfeit his or her life, while others cite religious doctrine to support their view that only God can take a human life. These arguments have remained essentially the same throughout the centuries. Likewise, the debate over euthanasia has persisted throughout the history of Western civilization. Supporters argue that it is compassionate to end the suffering of the dying by hastening their impending death; opponents insist that it is society's duty to make the dying as comfortable as possible as death takes its natural course.

Greenhaven Press's The History of Issues series illustrates this constancy of arguments surrounding major social issues. Each volume in the series focuses on one issue—including terrorism, the death penalty, and euthanasia—and examines how the debates have both evolved and remained essentially the same over the years. Primary documents such as newspaper articles, speeches, and government reports illuminate historical developments and offer perspectives from throughout history. Secondary sources provide overviews and commentaries from a more contemporary perspective. An introduction begins each anthology and supplies essential context and background. An annotated table of contents, chronology, and index allow for easy reference, and a bibliography and list of organizations to contact point to additional sources of information on the book's topic. With these features, The History of Issues series permits readers to glimpse both the historical and contemporary dimensions of humanity's most pressing and controversial social issues.

Introduction

Since the Supreme Court handed down its *Roe v. Wade* decision legalizing abortion in 1973, activists on both sides of the issue have battled in the courts, in the media, and in the streets. According to some social commentators, abortion is the single most contentious issue in America. These analysts contend that no other issue has generated such lasting diversity of opinion, and they believe that the debate has grown even more vociferous with the passing of time. The late Carl Sagan—astronomer, scientist, and political activist—neatly summed up the nature of the abortion controversy:

> The issue had been decided years ago. The court had chosen the middle ground. You'd think the fight was over. Instead, there are mass rallies, bombings and intimidation, murders of workers at abortion clinics, arrests, intense lobbying, legislative drama, Congressional hearings, Supreme Court decisions, major political parties almost defining themselves on the issue, and clerics threatening politicians with perdition. Partisans fling accusations of hypocrisy and murder. The intent of the Constitution and the will of God are equally invoked. Doubtful arguments are trotted out as certitudes. The contending factions call on science to bolster their positions. Families are divided, husbands and wives agree not to discuss it, old friends are no longer speaking. Politicians check the latest polls to discover the dictates of their consciences. Amid all the shouting, it is hard for the adversaries to hear one another. Opinions are polarized. Minds are closed.[1]

Former surgeon general Dr. C. Everett Koop observed, "Nothing like [this issue] has separated our society since the days of slavery."[2]

Curiously, however, although the common perception is that there are only two, highly opposed sides to the issue—

pro-choice (favoring abortion) and pro-life (against abortion)—polls indicate that most Americans actually take a middle stance. For example, a 2005 Gallup poll found that most Americans believe in the general right to abortion but support restrictions under some circumstances. Respondents were asked whether they think abortion should be legal under any circumstances, legal only under certain circumstances, or illegal in all circumstances. Twenty-six percent responded that abortion should always be legal, 56 percent believed it should be legal under certain circumstances, and 16 percent felt it should always be illegal. Only 2 percent responded as being unsure.[3] The relatively small percentage of respondents who represent the extreme ends of the abortion debate—that it should always be legal or always be illegal—seems to belie the commonly held belief, articulated by Sagan and Koop, that Americans are deeply divided over abortion.

This apparent disjunction between common wisdom about the divisiveness of the issue and the reality of how most Americans feel about it can be seen in the debate over embryonic stem cell research, an issue that has moved to the center of the abortion debate in recent years.

Scientists believe that embryonic stem cell research (ESCR) has the potential to lead to cures for many common diseases, including cancer and Parkinson's disease, that are the result of cellular dysfunction. During the procedure, scientists use stem cells—primitive cells that have the potential to grow into most kinds of tissues within the human body—to replace damaged or diseased tissues. Embryonic stem cell research has become central to the abortion debate because embryonic stem cells are harvested from embryos, which during the process are destroyed. Ardent pro-life supporters believe that using embryos in this fashion is tantamount to murdering human lives and is no different from abortion. On the surface it would seem that all people opposed to abortion would also object to ESCR, but increasingly that has not been the case.

Indeed, many abortion opponents have begun supporting ESCR research in large part because they have had personal experience with one of the many diseases that scientists hope to cure using ESCR. Going through a serious illness themselves or watching a loved one die as a result of a debilitating disease has prompted many abortion opponents to view this research in a more positive light. They have come to believe that saving the lives of people already living is a stronger obligation than protecting the lives of the unborn. The great shift of this segment of the population on the issue has resulted in a majority of Americans supporting ESCR. Carl Golden, press secretary to former Republican governors Tom Kean and Christine Whitman, explains the general feeling Americans have about ESCR:

> Support for stem-cell research is rooted not in ideology, but in a belief that scientific inquiry properly controlled and conducted in accordance with the highest moral values holds enormous benefit for humankind. Public opinion surveys have shown nearly seven in 10 Americans favor stem-cell research. It's not because 70 percent of Americans share an ideology; it's because 70 percent of Americans have faith in the integrity and dedication of scientists and physicians involved in the research. It's because 70 percent of Americans share a hope that eventual success—no matter how long it takes—will spare them and their loved ones the agony and despair brought on by such frightening ailments as Alzheimer's and Parkinson's disease.[4]

As the growing support for embryonic stem cell research shows, abortion is not a simple, two-sided issue. Most Americans grappling with the complexities of abortion seem to take a middle position, endorsing abortion but also supporting restrictions on the procedure. As seen in the case of ESCR, the majority of Americans seem to have decided that the lives of people already alive outweigh the potential life represented in embryonic cells.

Nonetheless, although polls indicate a consensus, obviously most people continue to feel deeply ambivalent about abortion. Individuals struggle to understand the ethical nature of abortion, whether it is good or bad for women, and whether it harms or benefits society. Many Americans continue to wonder when life begins—whether a cluster of cells is a human life or whether humanness occurs at some other stage of development. The conflict over abortion, then, seems to occur to a large degree in the minds of individuals struggling to understand how they should view this ethically complex issue. To be sure, polls suggest that the majority of Americans support abortion, but the increasing restrictions on the procedure are clear evidence that most people are still conflicted about it.

In the meantime, while most Americans' opinions on abortion lie somewhere in the middle, ardent abortion opponents and supporters continue to fuel the debate. In some respects, the tenacity of their positions is understandable. Each side recognizes that if it concedes any issue, it has stepped onto a slippery slope. If, for example, pro-life supporters concede that embryonic stem cell research is allowable, then what comes next? What will be the next exception pressed upon them? For many, taking a hard line avoids what they see as the moral gray area in which the majority of Americans seem to find themselves. By not giving any ground, they avoid the ethical confusion that others struggle with in deciding under what circumstances abortion is moral and beneficial to society.

The abortion controversy is thus difficult to characterize. It is in many ways defined by the extremes on both sides, but portraying the debate as simply two-sided ignores the majority of Americans who do not support these extreme positions. The majority of the debate seems to occur within individuals, making it difficult to find the pulse of how Americans really feel about abortion. As the history of the controversy shows, both the ardent opponents and supporters, and the majority in the middle, have helped determine abortion's fate. Activists have marched on Washington, killed abortion doctors, donated hundreds of thousands of dollars to get bills passed in Congress, and organized themselves into powerful organizations. Meanwhile, most Americans have quietly made up or changed their minds about the issue and have used the ballot box to vote for or against abortion restrictions. Many women have had to decide whether or not to opt for abortion when an unwanted pregnancy occurs. The difficulty that most people have in answering the questions "Is abortion ethical, and does it benefit society?" ensures that the controversy will continue to be played out in the public sphere and within the minds of individuals.

Notes

1. Carl Sagan and Ann Druyan, *Billions and Billions*. New York: Ballantine, 1997, pp. 163–64.
2. Quoted in Dick Bohrer, "Deception-on-Demand," *Moody Monthly*, May 1980, p. 27.
3. CNN.com, "Poll: Americans Back Abortion Limits, Oppose Ban," November 27, 2005. www.cnn.com/2005/US/11/27/abortion.poll.
4. Carl Golden, "Voice of Reason Against Far-Right Ideology," *Bergen Record*, August 2, 2005.

CHAPTER 1

Rights and Constitutionality

Chapter Preface

A visual time line of abortion laws would show an erratic progression, with liberal abortion laws being replaced by increased restrictions, then restrictions giving way to liberalization, which eventually gives way to more restrictions. The time line starts at the nation's founding, when the United States had no laws regulating abortion, preferring instead to follow English common law. English common law had no prohibition against abortion until "quickening," when the mother began to feel the baby's movement in her womb. However, by the mid-1800s many states had begun passing laws that restricted abortions under more narrowly defined criteria. These laws were passed because many people objected to abortion, although for varied reasons. Religious groups believed that the practice was an affront to God and that human life should never be destroyed. Many physicians objected to abortion because they resented the intense competition from non-physician abortion providers.

Both religious and physician groups used the political system to push for legislation to make abortion a criminal offense. The most notorious law enacted in the nineteenth century was the 1873 Comstock Law. Under the guise of outlawing pornography, the Comstock Law specifically prohibited the distribution of any printed material containing information about birth control or abortion. Individual states began enacting their own versions of the federal Comstock Law, and by 1900 every state in the union had laws that prohibited abortion under any circumstances.

Not until the 1965 Supreme Court ruling on *Griswold v. Connecticut* established a constitutional right to privacy did abortion begin to shed its criminal status. Most states began allowing abortion if medical necessity could be proved, but abortion rights activists began ratcheting up their efforts to make abortion legal under broader circumstances. The climax of the abortion rights movement came in 1973 with the Supreme Court's ruling on *Roe v. Wade*, which held that restrictions on abortion violated the Fourteenth Amendment's assertion of the right to privacy. A huge victory for abortion rights activists and a crushing defeat for the antiabortion movement, the Court's decision set the stage for years of legal wrangling.

Since the *Roe v. Wade* decision, the abortion debate has escalated, with pro-choice and pro-life advocates staunchly defending their positions. Each group continues to use the courts to try to advance its cause, and each has had its share of victories and defeats. The 1992 *Planned Parenthood v. Casey* Supreme Court decision upheld *Roe v. Wade*, but it allowed states to place certain restrictions on abortion—a kind of victory for both sides. In 2003 President George W. Bush signed into law a ban on partial-birth abortions, but federal courts have challenged it.

Today the Supreme Court has its first new members in more than a decade. Both sides of the abortion debate are gearing up for new battles. To be sure, these battles will continue to be waged in the courts, and the constitutionality of abortion will be tested again and again. It seems likely that the time line will continue as erratically as before, with both sides registering both victories and defeats.

U.S. Abortion Laws During the 1800s

Patricia G. Miller

In the following selection Patricia G. Miller traces the history of abortion laws in the United States from 1800, when no abortion laws existed, to the end of the nineteenth century, when every state in the union had adopted laws restricting abortion. Miller describes how the medical community, in particular the American Medical Association, was instrumental in promoting laws to regulate abortion. She theorizes that the physicians' primary goal was to eliminate competition from nondoctor abortion providers, and she concludes that much of their success in restricting abortion resulted from joining forces with the religious community, which believed that abortion was immoral. Miller is an abortion-rights activist and an attorney in the Pittsburgh, Pennsylvania, Court of Common Pleas Family Division.

Abortion in the United States has made a number of journeys from legality to criminalization and back again. In 1800 there were no abortion statutes at all in the United States. By 1900 every state in the union had laws prohibiting abortion for virtually any reason.

In colonial times and in the first quarter of the nineteenth century, Americans simply followed English common law in this matter, as in many others. Common law drew a distinction based on "quickening," the point during pregnancy when the woman can actually feel fetal movement. Although it varies from woman to woman, and even for the same woman from pregnancy to pregnancy, quickening generally occurs at about twenty weeks, the midpoint of pregnancy. Under common law, there were no prohibitions against abortion prior to

Patricia G. Miller, *The Worst of Times*. New York: HarperCollins, 1993. Copyright © 1993 by Patricia G. Miller. All rights reserved. Reproduced by permission.

quickening, and women could and did terminate their pregnancies if they chose to do so. Abortion after quickening was a crime, but it was a lesser crime than manslaughter or murder, and the penalties were much less severe.

Home medical manuals of the day routinely provided abortion information. [William] Buchan's *Domestic Medicine* (1816) suggested several courses of action to restore menses following a missed period, among them bloodletting and taking quinine or tincture of hellebore, a violent gastrointestinal poison. Later in the book, the author warned the reader about certain common "causes" of abortion, including vigorous exercise, jumping, falling, and blows to the belly, as well as severe vomiting. . . .

Demand for Abortion Increased

In the nineteenth century, many observers maintained that only single women desperate to hide the "shame" of nonmarital sex were having abortions, but this argument crumbled in the 1840s. The growing number of abortion providers and the proliferation of abortion home remedies and patent medicines made it abundantly clear—in an era of poor to nonexistent contraception—that white, married, upper-middle-class, native-born Protestant American women were resorting to abortions to delay childbearing or limit the number of children they had.

By the 1840s, because of increased demand, abortion—the only existing birth control measure known to be effective—had become an American medical specialty, a service publicly traded in the free market by recognized practitioners, most of whom were not doctors. As had been the case during the preceding forty years with other medical services, there was intense competition between "real doctors" and these lay practitioners, or "irregular doctors." At the time, there was great variation in the training and competence of medical practitioners. In 1800 two-thirds of the "doctors" in Philadelphia were not graduates of any medical school. In rural areas faith healers, midwives, and folk doctors took care of the medical needs of the community, including uncomplicated surgery. And even medical school graduates were not necessarily qualified physicians. Before 1860 most American medical schools competed aggressively for paying students, without regard to their intelligence or abilities. Few applicants were denied admission, since in a very real sense their tuition kept the doors open. Some of these schools were nothing more than diploma mills. If you paid your money, you got one.

One of the most prominent nineteenth-century abortionists was Madame Restell, of 148 Greenwich Street in New York City. She was so successful that she had branch offices at 7 Essex Street in Boston and 7 South Seventh Street in Philadelphia, as well as an army of door-to-door salesmen who peddled her "female monthly pills."

Home Remedies Abounded

At a time when there was no federal regulation of medicines, patent medicines promising miracle cures for an assortment of human ailments were openly advertised in the classified sections of newspapers, through handbills and flyers, and by word of mouth. "Female monthly pills," "renovating pills," and "lunar pills" were vague but popular remedies for such conditions as "irregular" menses, or, in a somewhat more accurate description, "obstructed" or "suppressed" menses. In case the potential user still had not caught on, the small print on the label contained a "warning" that married women who might be pregnant should not take the pills, since they were "sure to produce a miscarriage."

How effective these home remedies and patent medicines were is not known. Indeed, it's difficult even to speculate, since the patent medicines were not required to describe their contents. What we do know is that there was a lively interest in, and market for, products believed capable of correcting "suppressed" menses.

Madame Restell's pills were guaranteed to cure the "suppression problem." To accommodate those not within reach of her door-to-door salesmen, she advertised that the pills could be mailed anywhere in the country. The reader was cautioned to beware of imitation monthly pills—the genuine article bore Madame's signature on each box. Madame Restell, whose real name was Ann Lohman, also had facilities to "board ladies overnight," should their condition require it.

Many abortion practitioners billed themselves as doctors, but their actual medical training is not known. In January 1845, the *Boston Times* carried the ad of one Dr. Carswell, who treated such female complaints as "suppressions." A Dr. Dow advertised "good accommodations for ladies," and a Dr. Kurtz treated "private diseases." Female abortionists tended to prefer the title "Madame"—Madame Drunette, Madame Costello, Madame Carson, and Madame Moor gave Madame Restell plenty of competition—though they often added "ladies' physician" or "ladies' doctress" in advertising their services.

Doctors Tried to Control Abortion

Abortion was a highly visible and profitable industry by the middle of the nineteenth century, although the earnings of individual abortionists, whether medical doctors or lay practitioners, probably varied greatly. The demand for abortion was also substantial enough to sustain several supporting industries. For example, by 1850 the manufacture of abortifacients had become a significant part of the drug industry. In 1871 it was estimated that sales of abortifacients surpassed the million-dollar mark. The profits were sufficient to convince Parke Davis and Company to engage in the wholesale manufacture of abortifacients called Emmenagogue and Emmenagogue Improved. In 1871 Madame Restell was reported to have been spending sixty thousand dollars a year on advertising alone.

By mid-century the medical community had begun a concerted effort to improve, professionalize, and ultimately control the practice of medicine in the United States. In line with that goal, doctors increasingly took the view that abortion at any time was to be avoided. Some doctors may have objected to the profits being enjoyed by the "irregulars," but the primary motivation of the medical establishment was probably the undisputed fact that in this era, some twenty years before Joseph Lister introduced modern antiseptic surgery—abortion, childbirth, and surgical procedures of any sort were hazardous undertakings. Thus, discouraging or even outlawing what could be considered "elective surgery" would surely save lives.

If doctors were to succeed in stamping out abortion, they had to convince women to reject it. Though health concerns provided the most compelling argument, some doctors began to denounce abortion as "morally reprehensible" as well as medically unsafe. It was a short step from "reprehensible" and "disreputable" to "damnable," "evil," "abominable," and finally "unnatural." It mattered little whether women rejected abortion because they thought it was dangerous or because they thought it was wrong, just so long as they rejected it.

Doctors began to organize against the commercialization of abortion, which they called "Restellism" after their best-known irregular competitor, and to lobby state legislatures for new restrictive laws. Some of these laws were apparently designed to protect women, like the legislation common in the early part of the century, but more followed the "regular doctor" model intended to drive commercial abortionists out of business, along with pharmacists who prescribed their own abortifacients and any other non-physicians who might be involved in the abortion decision and implementation.

New Laws Tightened Restrictions

The medical community was successful in getting a stronger anti-abortion law passed in New York in 1846. The law ignored the quickening distinction and made it a crime for anyone—doctor or not—to "administer" to or "prescribe" for a pregnant woman with regard to abortion, or even to "advise" her on the subject—a provision that implicated even family members and friends. New York's law went a step beyond any previous legislation in making the woman herself liable for prosecution. However, because women were still viewed as victims by society if not by the law, this provision was evidently not enforced.

In 1847, for the first time anywhere, Massachusetts made it a crime for an abortionist to advertise publicly. At around the same time, there was concern about the falling birth rate; the Massachusetts ban, it was hoped, would check the dissemination of information about abortion, still the only reliable form of contraception. Soon five more states (Virginia in 1848, California, New Hampshire, New Jersey, and Wisconsin in 1849) enacted anti-abortion laws that reflected the growing opposition—and power—of the medical community.

This major crusade by physicians to squelch their competitors lasted until 1880. Prior to the formation of the American Medical Association in 1847, opposition to abortion was scattered and largely ineffective. The "regulars" associated with the AMA quickly got their feet under them, and by the beginning of the Civil War, they had launched an aggressive anti-abortion campaign. Once the AMA came to speak for a large part of the "respectable" medical community, it became a force capable of controlling abortion policy in the United States.

The AMA was steadfastly committed to outlawing the "irregulars" and the pharmacists while saving the "therapeutic exception" for themselves. After all, who could tell better than a "real doctor" when the continuation of a pregnancy was life-threatening? Between 1860 and 1880 the AMA's campaign to criminalize abortion began to have measurable results. Home medical guides, which had once discussed abortion techniques openly, were now silent or mentioned them only to condemn them. In the end, the AMA's effort to outlaw virtually all abortions met with total success. Their effort to drive the non-doctor abortionists out of business, on the other hand, did not. The abortionists simply went underground—a result as ironic as it was unintended. Now, with abortion illegal, it was mainly the underground abortionists, not the doctors, who were performing the procedure. One hundred years later the AMA, speaking *amicus curiae* [friend of the court] in the 1970s court challenges to these same restrictive laws, spoke eloquently and persuasively of the compelling medical need to legalize abortion so that it would be safe.

The AMA was not solely responsible for the first wave of laws outlawing abortion. Some segments of organized religion, Protestant as well as Catholic, began to speak out about the "evils" of abortion. In 1869 Bishop Spaulding of Baltimore set forth what was to remain the official Catholic position for the next hundred years: "No mother is allowed, under any circumstances, to permit the death of her unborn infant, not even for the sake of preserving her own life." More influential, because of their greater numbers, were the Protestant denominations opposing abortion. Many Protestants feared that they would not keep up with the reproductive rates of Catholic immigrants, who tended to be opposed to both contraception and abortion. A leading Congregationalist characterized abortion as "fashionable murder." The Presbyterians adopted a national resolution calling abortion "murder" and "a crime against God and nature."

The Comstock Law Drove Abortion Underground

In the 1870s Anthony Comstock's anti-obscenity movement

gave the foes of abortion the final boost they needed for complete success in criminalizing abortion. Comstock was head of the New York Society for the Suppression of Vice. In 1873 he was sufficiently powerful to persuade Congress to pass an "Act for the Suppression of Trade in and Circulation of Obscene Literature and Articles of Immoral Use," allegedly intended to suppress the traffic in pornography. Under that law, it became a federal offense to sell, offer to sell, give away, offer to give away, or even possess with the intent to give away, a book, pamphlet, paper, advertisement, or anything else of "indecent or immoral nature." A similar ban extended to contraceptive devices and to any article or medicine that would cause an abortion, unless prescribed by a "physician in good standing"—a provision that gave doctors a powerful boost in their efforts to suppress their lay competitors. The law also made it a federal crime to write or print or cause to be written *any* information about how to obtain "obscene or indecent" articles or how to get an abortion.

"Comstockery," as it came to be called, did more than anything else to drive abortion underground, where it was to remain for nearly one hundred years. Comstock himself became a special agent of the federal government, charged with enforcing the act's provisions. In the 1870s he was the leading abortionist-hunter in the United States, basing his prosecutions primarily on charges of illegal advertising. In 1878 he arrested Madame Restell after buying an abortifacient from her. She committed suicide before her trial, making Comstock a hero in the crusade against abortion.

Prohibition Becomes Absolute

Between 1860 and 1880 a burst of legislative activity produced at least forty new anti-abortion statutes, thirteen of them in states that had never had anti-abortion laws. Most fostered the medical establishment's goal of absolute prohibition, under virtually all circumstances, no matter what the method, at any stage of pregnancy. Pennsylvania's abortion law, passed in 1860, made attempted abortion a crime even if the woman wasn't really pregnant. These new statutes made the woman liable, along with the abortionist and any advertiser or other provider of information. During this period, married women who desired to limit family size were said to be avoiding the responsibilities of married life and even to be living in a state of "legalized prostitution."

States, often led by their medical societies, began enacting their own anti-pornography "Comstock laws" to prevent publication of "obscene" advertisements. Aimed at the commercial abortionist, most of these laws had an anti-abortifacient clause as well. By 1880 the quickening distinction had all but disappeared from state anti-abortion laws, women seeking abortions were no longer victims but criminals, and the dissemination of any kind of abortion information was a crime. A decade later every state had an anti-abortion law.

By the turn of the century, most traditional physicians had been taught Lister's antiseptic techniques, so surgery and childbirth were immeasurably safer. So too would abortion have been if it had not disappeared from the open market. The medical community and the larger society had fallen under the spell of their own illusions. It was commonly believed that most women had been "educated" to reject abortion; that married women, conspicuous consumers fifty years earlier, had seen the error of their ways; and that only the unwilling victims of seduction, impregnated and then abandoned, sought abortions.

Conveniently, it seemed that the demand for abortion had disappeared at about the same time as the abortionists themselves. But the demand was by no means gone. Abortionists and unwillingly pregnant women had simply been driven underground, where they would remain, hidden and silent, for the next seventy years.

The Comstock Law Outlaws Abortion Information

Margaret Sanger

Born in 1879, Margaret Sanger was a nurse who, in her work with poor women, saw firsthand the effects of unplanned and unwelcome pregnancies. She is credited with inventing the term birth control. In the following selection Sanger decries the results of the 1873 Comstock Law, which prohibited the publication of any material containing information about birth control or abortion because such information was considered obscene. Sanger charges that the Comstock Law was merely a ruse for persecuting poor women who sought family-planning advice. She concludes that the need for abortion increased after the law took effect because women were denied the ability to control the size of their families through birth control.

There is nothing which causes so much laughter or calls forth so many joking comments by people in Europe as Comstockery in America. Our English cousins have a vague idea of its intricacies but the Latin mind, either Italian, French or Spanish, cannot grasp the idea of its existence.

America stands in the eyes of the younger generations of the various countries of Europe as a great hope and inspiration for the development of a free race. What, then, is their surprise and disappointment to learn that an American woman, born on American soil, must leave the "land of the free and home of the brave" to escape imprisonment for discussing the subject of Family Limitation.

When the Latin hears this he storms and rages and asks where the integrity of manhood has gone, that it will allow such an infringement on one's personal liberty.

Margaret Sanger, "Comstockery in America," *International Socialist Review*, July 1915, pp. 46–49.

But the English calmly shake their heads and tell you that the same issue was fought out in London in 1877 when [birth control advocates] Annie Besant and Charles Bradlaugh braved the courts and won freedom in their cause for British subjects for all time. They will tell you they sympathize, but can do little to help you, for the place to fight "Comstockery in America" is in America.

There is no doubt of the truth of this assertion, so in order to fight Comstockery we must know who and what is behind it and put a strong searchlight on actions, which are considered by all classes of people throughout the civilized world as most contemptible and despicable.

Anthony Comstock's Influence

Anthony Comstock was born in 1844. He has been Secretary and Special Agent for the Society for the Suppression of Vice since 1873; also U. S. Post Office Inspector since the same year. He records that he has destroyed 160 tons of literature and brought 3,760 "criminals" to "justice" during these years.

There is no doubt in the minds of thinking people that the influence of the Church in America has gradually been declining since the days of [agnostic] Robert Ingersoll and that today, as a power, it has almost entirely collapsed. But the relentless war which Ingersoll waged against the Church and the present-day power of Comstock are somewhat connected: the Church feeling its power going from it, through Ingersoll's influence, grasped at the straw held out to it by the Government, called the "Comstock laws." These were passed in 1873, and prohibit the sending of any matter through the mails which, in the opinion of Anthony Comstock, the Postal Authorities choose to call "obscene."

Thus, the Church, hiding behind the closed doors of the suppression of Vice Society, works its timid and poisonous way through the Government via its special agent, Comstock.

The passing of the Comstock laws in 1873 was designed to aid and abet both moral and religious prejudice and persecutions. This aroused the wrath of the freethinking and liberty-loving populace, and in 1878 great agitation was aroused against these laws: a petition was presented to Congress, headed by the name of Robert G. Ingersoll and signed by 70,000 "freemen," requesting the repeal of these outrageous laws. They were passed and executed ostensibly to prevent the passage of obscene literature through the U. S. mails, but actually were designed and enforced to destroy the liberty of conscience and thought in matters of religion and against the freedom of the press.

The petition caused great agitation and aroused so much interest that a few years later the law was revised, removing the interference of religious prejudice, but the moral interference was left and Anthony Comstock then became the official guardian of American morality.

Violaters Were Arrested

Since that power was entrusted to Comstock, it was most natural that he should "make good" and give some evidence of the need of his special service.

This he proves by sending out his minions of agents (Government spies) to tempt obscure booksellers to sell him a prohibited book. One case on record is of a father and son, running a book store in the lower East Side of New York City. The agents came again and again asking for a certain medical book. The father stated that he did not have it, and the agent then induced him to order one for him. The father, thinking there was a demand for the book, sent to the publisher and purchased a copy, which the Agent called for the following day, paid for it and turned round and arrested the bookseller. He was dragged off to court and was sentenced to one year in Blackwell's Island. The son was also fined, and as I have not

Leader of the birth control movement, Margaret Sanger, waits to testify before a Senate subcommittee on whether physicians should make birth control available to their patients. Library of Congress

the records here with me, I can not say if he was not also imprisoned.

The case of Moses Harmon is familiar to all. This man of seventy years, residing in Chicago, editing the paper "Lucifer," in which he discussed birth control and kindred subjects, was arrested six or seven times, sentenced to imprisonment year after year, always resuming the fight when he came from prison, until finally his health gave way through his sufferings and imprisonment, and he died, a victim of Comstock persecution.

There have been many publications during these years which have been suppressed by the orders of Comstock, and the publisher imprisoned, but one of the latest, and most flagrant disregard of Press Freedom was in the suppression and confiscation of the monthly publication, "The Woman Rebel." This was a working woman's paper, the first of its kind ever issued in America. It had for its motto: "Working Women, build up within yourselves a conscious fighting character against all things which enslave you," and claimed that one of the working woman's greatest enslavements was her ignorance of the means to control the size of her family. The editor promised to defy the existing law and to impart such information to the readers of "The Woman Rebel" and urged all working women to rally to its support.

The first issue in March, 1914, was suppressed. The May, July, August, September and October issues were suppressed and confiscated, and three indictments, on the March, May and July issues, covering twelve counts, were returned against me, as the editor, by the Federal Grand Jury. One of the counts against me was for an article called "Open Discussion." This was a discussion of the subject of birth control and was considered "obscene." Another was an article announcing the organization of The Birth Control League, setting forth its object and methods of organization. All the indictments were returned and counts were made on all articles which discussed the idea of the Working Woman keeping down the number of her family.

The Publication Advocated Economic Freedom

"The Woman Rebel" did not advocate the practice of this knowledge as a "panacea" for the present economic enslavement, but it did urge the practice of it as the most important immediate step which should be taken toward the economic emancipation of the workers. Thousands of letters poured in to me from all over the country. I was besieged with requests for the information from all kinds and classes of people. Nearly every letter agreed with me that too long have the workers produced the slave class, the children for the mills, the soldiers for the wars, and the time had come to watch the masters produce their own slaves if they must have them. We know the capitalist class must have a slave class, bred in poverty and reared in ignorance. That is why it is quite consistent with their laws that there should be a heavy penalty of five years' imprisonment for imparting information as to the means of preventing conception. Industry in the U.S.A. is fairly new; it is reaching out in foreign lands to capture trade and to undersell its rival competitors. They have only one way to do this, and that is to get labor cheap. The cheapest labor is that of women and children; the larger the number of children in a family, the earlier they enter the factory. We need only to look to our mill towns to see the truth of this statement; so the conditions in the cotton mills of the South where little boys and girls, eight, nine and ten years of age, wend their sleepy way to the mills in the morning before the winter sun has risen, to work at a killing tension for twelve hours as helper to the mother, and return again when the sun has set.

We, who know the conditions there, know that the father cannot get a man's wage, because a child's labor can be had.

There is an average of nine children to every family in these and in other industrial sections where child labor exists and wages run low and infant mortality runs high.

Many of the stockholders of these mills are legislators and congressmen who have to do with the making of the laws. Naturally it is to their interest that child slaves be born into the world and their duty is to enforce the laws to that end.

"The Woman Rebel" told the Working Woman these things, and told her that a large family of children is one of the greatest obstacles in the way to obtain economic freedom for her class. It is the greatest burden to them in all ways, for no matter how spirited and revolutionary one may feel, the piteous cry of hunger of several little ones will compel a man to forego the future good of his class to the present need of his family.

It is the man with a large family who is so often the burden of a strike. He is usually the hardest to bring out on strike, for it is he and his who suffer the most through its duration. Everywhere, in the shop, in the army of the unemployed, in the bread line where men are ready to take the place of a striker, it is the large family problem which is the chief of the multitudes of miseries confront[ing] the working class today.

Need for Abortion Remained Constant

"The Woman Rebel" told the Working Woman that there is no freedom for her until she has this knowledge which will enable her to say if she will become a mother or not. The fewer children she had to cook, wash and toil for, the more leisure she would have to read, think and develop. That freedom demands leisure, and her first freedom must be in her right of herself over her own body; the right to say what she will do with it in marriage and out of it; the right to become a mother, or not, as she desires and sees fit to do; that all these rights swing around the pivot of the means to prevent conception, and every woman had the right to have this knowledge if she wished it.

As editor and publisher of "The Woman Rebel," I felt a great satisfaction and inspiration in the response which came from working men and women all over America. For fourteen years I have been much in the nursing field, and know too well the intolerable conditions among the workers which a large family does not decrease.

I saw that the working women ask for this knowledge to prevent bringing more children into the world, and saw the medical profession shake its head in silence at this request.

I saw that the women of wealth obtain this information with little difficulty, while the working man's wife must continue to bring children into the world she could not feed or clothe, or else resort to an abortion.

I saw that it was the working class women who fill the death list which results from abortion, for though the women of wealth have abortions performed too, there is given them the best medical care and attention money can buy; trained nurses watch over them, and there is seldom any evil consequence. But the working woman must look for the cheapest assistance. The professional abortionist, the unclean midwives, the fake and quack—all feed upon her helplessness and thrive and prosper on her ignorance. It is the Comstock laws which produce the abortionist and make him a thriving necessity while the lawmakers close their Puritan eyes.

Griswold v. Connecticut Extended the Right to Privacy Too Far

Robert P. George and David L. Tubbs

In 1961 Estelle Griswold was convicted of illegally operating a birth control clinic in New Haven, Connecticut. In a landmark ruling by the Supreme Court in 1965, her conviction was overturned, and Connecticut's law prohibiting the use of contraceptives by married couples was ruled unconstitutional. Griswold v. Connecticut *established a broad right to privacy and set the framework for* Roe v. Wade *(1973), which legalized abortion. In* Roe *the court ruled that abortion could not be banned because such a law would violate a woman's right to privacy. In the following selection Robert P. George and David L. Tubbs argue that the* Griswold *decision was flawed because it asserted a right to privacy that is not in fact stipulated in the Constitution. George and Tubbs contend that* Griswold *set a precedent for other flawed decisions such as* Roe. *George is a professor of jurisprudence at Princeton University. He is the author of* In Defense of Natural Law. *Tubbs is an assistant professor of political science at King's College, New York.*

Forty years ago [in 1965], in *Griswold v. Connecticut*, the Supreme Court of the United States struck down state laws forbidding the sale, distribution, and use of contraceptives on the basis of a novel constitutional doctrine known as the "right to marital privacy."

At the time, the decision appeared to be harmless. After all, *Griswold* simply allowed married couples to decide whether to use contraceptives. But the Supreme Court soon trans-

Robert P. George and David L. Tubbs, "The Bad Decision That Started It All," *National Review,* July 18, 2005, pp. 29–40. Copyright © 2005 by the National Review, Inc., 215 Lexington Ave., New York, NY 10016. Reproduced by permission.

formed the "right to privacy" (the reference to marriage quickly disappeared) into a powerful tool for making public policy. In *Eisenstadt v. Baird* (1972), the Court changed a right of *spouses*—justified in *Griswold* precisely by reference to the importance of marriage—into a right of *unmarried* adults to buy and use contraceptives. Then, in a move that plunged the United States into a "culture war," the Court ruled in *Roe v. Wade* and *Doe v. Bolton* (1973) that this generalized "right to privacy" also encompassed a woman's virtually unrestricted right to have an abortion.

Privacy and the Constitution

No one doubts that there are true privacy rights in the Constitution, especially in the Fourth Amendment, which protects against unreasonable searches and seizures and ensures that warrants issue only upon a showing of probable cause that a crime has been committed. (Indeed, these rights prevented any kind of aggressive enforcement of the laws struck down in *Griswold*.) But the justices in *Griswold* produced a non-text-based and generalized right. "Privacy" functioned as a euphemism for immunity from those public-morals laws deemed by the justices to reflect benighted moral views.

The privacy decisions that sprang from *Griswold* have been widely criticized, and in the last 20 years there have been two notable efforts to silence and stigmatize that criticism. The first occurred in 1987, when a coalition of liberal interest groups helped to scotch Judge Robert Bork's nomination to the Supreme Court, partly because of Bork's misgivings about this novel doctrine. The second occurred in 1992, when the Supreme Court decided *Planned Parenthood v. Casey*, which reaffirmed the "central holding" of *Roe v. Wade*.

Neither of these efforts succeeded. To this day, millions of Americans cannot accept *Roe v. Wade* as constitutionally legitimate. And thanks to recent developments, public suspicion of the Court's "privacy" doctrine is now greater than ever.

[In 2003], in *Lawrence v. Texas*, the Supreme Court pushed the doctrine into new territory by overruling *Bowers v. Hardwick* (1986), a decision that had upheld a state's authority to prohibit homosexual sodomy. But in *Lawrence*, Justice Anthony Kennedy provocatively remarked that *Bowers* was wrong the day it was decided. Criticism of the ruling in *Lawrence* intensified a few months later when the supreme judicial court of Massachusetts promulgated a right to same-sex marriage in that state. In *Goodridge v. Department of Public Health* (2003), the court cited *Lawrence* to support this newly minted right. It evidently mattered little to these judges that the majority opinion in *Lawrence* expressly denied that the case involved the issue of marriage.

As the courts push the "privacy" doctrine further and further, public criticism keeps pace. *Griswold*, however, has received little attention. Even harsh critics of *Roe* and *Lawrence* are loath to say that *Griswold* was wrongly decided. Most of those who worry about the judicial abuse of the right to privacy do not want or expect the Supreme Court to revisit the case. Yet the cogency of any serious critique of "privacy" may depend on the willingness to reexamine the roots of the doctrine in *Griswold*.

Consider abortion. Conceding the correctness of *Griswold* gives a huge advantage to the defenders of *Roe* and *Casey*. They benefit because so many influential jurists and scholars say that the "inner logic" of the contraception cases must yield something like *Roe*. Outsiders may regard this argument with skepticism, but its purpose is clear: It tries to smooth the road from *Griswold* to *Eisenstadt* to *Roe*—and beyond.

The Myths of *Griswold*

But one point is rarely mentioned. Even though *Griswold* was less consequential than *Roe*, the two cases suffer from similar flaws. The many shortcomings of *Griswold* are less well known, because the case is enveloped in myths.

In American law schools, decisions such as *Roe, Casey,* and *Lawrence* are widely praised—not because of their legal merits (which are dubious), but because they comport with the ideology of "lifestyle liberalism" that enjoys hegemony there. Consequently, since 1973 most legal scholars have had no incentive to reassess *Griswold.* But if *Griswold* was wrongly decided, *Roe*—intellectually shaky on any account—loses even the meager jurisprudential support on which it rests.

The lack of scholarly engagement with *Griswold* partly explains the myths now surrounding it. Exposing those myths further undermines the arguments for a generalized right to privacy.

Myth #1: The Connecticut laws were "purposeless restraints," serving no social interest. Supreme Court justice David Souter is one of several jurists to make this assertion. The confusion arises from *Griswold,* whose majority opinion nowhere identifies a legislative purpose.

For anyone who cares to look, the purposes of the laws are apparent in the record of the case: Connecticut sought to promote marital fidelity and stable families by discouraging attempts to avoid the possible consequences of non-marital sexual relations through the use of contraceptives. Prominent judges in Connecticut recognized the legitimacy of these purposes, and the state's supreme court upheld the laws against several constitutional challenges from 1940 to 1964.

Did Connecticut's policy go too far in its efforts to promote marital fidelity? Many thought so. But roughly 30 states regulated contraceptives in the early 1960s, and the uniqueness of Connecticut's statutory scheme was long recognized as its constitutional prerogative.

Myth #2: The decision in Griswold *rested on some overarching or time-honored constitutional principle.* Ostensibly, that principle was "privacy." But the *Griswold* doctrine would have been unrecognizable to the Supreme Court even a few years earlier. In *Gardner v. Massachusetts* (1938), for example, the Court dismissed a similar challenge, noting that the suit failed to present "a substantial federal question."

In the majority opinion in *Griswold*, Justice William O. Douglas referred—as comically metaphysical as it sounds—to "penumbras formed by emanations" of specific constitutional guarantees as the source of the new right. He had nothing else to go on.

Other jurists have since argued that the right to marital privacy could be derived from cases before 1965 involving the rights of parents to direct the upbringing of their children. But the cases they cite have little in common with *Griswold*.

What, then, was the operative "principle" in *Griswold?* Nothing other than the Court's desire to place its imprimatur on "enlightened" views about human sexuality. This project continued beyond *Griswold* and culminated in *Lawrence*, where the Court essentially said that all adults in America have a right to engage in consenting, non-marital sexual relations. Consistently missing from the Court's discourse on privacy, however, has been any discussion of parental duties, public health, and the welfare of children.

Myth #3: No sensible jurist or commentator would say that the case was wrongly decided. In fact, two widely respected and sensible jurists, Justices Hugo Black and Potter Stewart, dissented in *Griswold*. Black was a noted liberal and, like Stewart, recorded his opposition to Connecticut's policy as a political matter. Yet both jurists insisted that the policy was a valid exercise of the state's power to promote public health, safety, and morals.

To Justices Black and Stewart, the "right to privacy" cloaked a naked policy preference. Justices in the majority were, without constitutional warrant, substituting their own judgments for those of the elected representatives in Connecticut. This, according to jurists across the political spectrum, is precisely what had brought shame on the Court during the "Lochner era," from roughly 1890 to 1937, when in the name of an unwritten "liberty of contract" the justices invalidated state social-welfare and worker-protection laws. But the crucial distinction underscored by Black and Stewart between the desirability or justice of a policy and the state's constitutional authority to enact it lost much of its currency as the right to privacy expanded.

Myth #4: The legislation invalidated in Griswold might be widely used again if the case was overturned. This line was often repeated in 1987 when Robert Bork was nominated to the Supreme Court. Meant to frighten ordinary citizens who approve of contraceptive use, this scenario simply fails to acknowledge changes in public opinion since 1965. Laws like those struck down in *Griswold* clearly have little chance of passing today even in the most conservative states.

Myth #5: The widespread use of contraceptives in the United States today provides a post hoc justification for Griswold. When *Griswold* was decided, adults could buy and use contraceptives in almost every state (despite various regulations on their sale and distribution). Given the social ferment of the 1960s and '70s, the Connecticut policy would sooner or later have been modified. But the ubiquity of contraceptives in America today does not justify *Griswold*—any more than the widespread use of abortion justifies *Roe.*

Griswold Was a Colossal Mistake

It might seem fanciful to say that the idea of a generalized constitutional right to "privacy" could now be repudiated; many believe that it has become an integral part of American law. But no one should accept this conclusion. The struggle against usurpations by the Supreme Court committed under the pretext of giving effect to unwritten constitutional rights has a historical precedent. As noted, from roughly 1890 to

1937, the Supreme Court invalidated worker-protection and social-welfare legislation on the basis of an unenumerated right to "liberty of contract." After much criticism, the Court relented and in 1937 announced that it would defer to legislative judgment where policies did not run afoul of constitutional principles. They promised, in short, to halt the practice of reading into the Constitution their own personal judgments about social and economic policy and the morality of economic relations.

The Supreme Court will not revisit the question of state or federal laws banning contraceptives. Yet the Court can and should find an occasion to admit that the manipulation of constitutional law that began with *Griswold* has been a colossal mistake. Such an admission would hardly be radical or, as we have observed, unprecedented. The Court's confession of error in repudiating its *Griswold* jurisprudence, far from harming its reputation, would enhance its prestige. We have no doubt that the same good effect would redound to the Court if the justices were candidly to speak the truth: The idea of a generalized right to privacy floating in penumbras formed by emanations was a pure judicial invention—one designed to license the judicial usurpation of democratic legislative authority.

Two Supreme Court Justices Argue the Pros and Cons of *Roe v. Wade*

Harry Blackmun and William Rehnquist

Norma McCorvey, a pregnant single woman identified as Jane Roe, brought a class action suit against the state of Texas to challenge the constitutionality of its criminal abortion law. The law prohibited abortion except for the purpose of saving the life of the mother. On appeal, the case was heard by the U.S. Supreme Court, which handed down its decision on January 22, 1973. The Court, in a seven-to-two decision, ruled that Texas's criminal abortion law infringed on McCorvey's Ninth and Fourteenth Amendment right to privacy. The majority opinion was written by Justice Harry Blackmun while the dissenting opinion was written by Justice William Rehnquist. The following excerpt from the text of the decision includes both the majority ruling and the dissenting opinion.

The Majority Opinion

A pregnant single woman (Roe) brought a class action challenging the constitutionality of the Texas criminal abortion laws, which proscribe procuring or attempting an abortion except on medical advice for the purpose of saving the mother's life. A licensed physician (Hallford), who had two state abortion prosecutions pending against him, was permitted to intervene. A childless married couple (the Does), the wife not being pregnant, separately attacked the laws, basing alleged injury on the future possibilities of contraceptive failure, pregnancy, unpreparedness for parenthood, and impairment of the wife's health. A three-judge District Court, which consolidated

Harry Blackmun and William Rehnquist, opinions, *Roe v. Wade,* U.S. Supreme Court, January 22, 1973.

the actions, held that Roe and Hallford, and members of their classes, had standing to sue and presented justiciable controversies. Ruling that declaratory, though not injunctive, relief was warranted, the court declared the abortion statutes void as vague and overbroadly infringing those plaintiffs' Ninth and Fourteenth Amendment rights. The court ruled the Does' complaint not justiciable. Appellants directly appealed to this Court on the injunctive rulings, and appellee cross-appealed from the District Court's grant of declaratory relief to Roe and Hallford. Held:

1. While 28 U.S.C. 1253 authorizes no direct appeal to this Court from the grant or denial of declaratory relief alone, review is not foreclosed when the case is properly before the Court on appeal from specific denial of injunctive relief and the arguments as to both injunctive and declaratory relief are necessarily identical.

2. Roe has standing to sue; the Does and Hallford do not.

(a) Contrary to appellee's contention, the natural termination of Roe's pregnancy did not moot her suit. Litigation involving pregnancy, which is "capable of repetition, yet evading review," is an exception to the usual federal rule that an actual controversy must exist at review stages and not simply when the action is initiated.

(b) The District Court correctly refused injunctive, but erred in granting declaratory, relief to Hallford, who alleged no federally protected right not assertable as a defense against the good-faith state prosecutions pending against him.

(c) The Does' complaint, based as it is on contingencies, any one or more of which may not occur, is too speculative to present an actual case or controversy.

3. State criminal abortion laws, like those involved here, that except from criminality only a life-saving procedure on the mother's behalf without regard to the stage of her pregnancy and other interests involved violate the Due Process Clause of the Fourteenth Amendment, which protects against

state action the right to privacy, including a woman's qualified right to terminate her pregnancy. Though the State cannot override that right, it has legitimate interests in protecting both the pregnant woman's health and the potentiality of human life, each of which interests grows and reaches a "compelling" point at various stages of the woman's approach to term.

(a) For the stage prior to approximately the end of the first trimester, the abortion decision and its effectuation must be left to the medical judgment of the pregnant woman's attending physician.

(b) For the stage subsequent to approximately the end of the first trimester, the State, in promoting its interest in the health of the mother, may, if it chooses, regulate the abortion procedure in ways that are reasonably related to maternal health.

(c) For the stage subsequent to viability the State, in promoting its interest in the potentiality of human life, may, if it chooses, regulate, and even proscribe, abortion except where necessary, in appropriate medical judgment, for the preservation of the life or health of the mother.

4. The State may define the term "physician" to mean only a physician currently licensed by the State, and may proscribe any abortion by a person who is not a physician as so defined.

5. It is unnecessary to decide the injunctive relief issue since the Texas authorities will doubtless fully recognize the Court's ruling that the Texas criminal abortion statutes are unconstitutional.

[Justice Harry] Blackmun, delivered the opinion of the Court, in which Burger, C. J., and Douglas, Brennan, Stewart, Marshall, and Powell, JJ., joined. Burger, C. J., post, p. 207, Douglas, J., post, p. 209, and Stewart, J., post, p. 167, filed concurring opinions. White, J., filed a dissenting opinion, in which [Justice William] Rehnquist, joined, post, p. 221. Rehnquist, J., filed a dissenting opinion, post, p. 171. . . .

The Dissenting Opinion

The Court's opinion brings to the decision of this troubling question both extensive historical fact and a wealth of legal scholarship. While the opinion thus commands my respect, I find myself nonetheless in fundamental disagreement with those parts of it that invalidate the Texas statute in question, and therefore dissent.

The Court's opinion decides that a State may impose virtually no restriction on the performance of abortions during the first trimester of pregnancy. Our previous decisions indicate that a necessary predicate for such an opinion is a plaintiff who was in her first trimester of pregnancy at some time during the pendency of her law-suit. While a party may vindicate his own constitutional rights, he may not seek vindication for the rights of others. The Court's statement of facts in this case makes clear, however, that the record in no way indicates the presence of such a plaintiff. We know only that plaintiff Roe at the time of filing her complaint was a pregnant woman; for aught that appears in this record, she may have been in her last trimester of pregnancy as of the date the complaint was filed.

Nothing in the Court's opinion indicates that Texas might not constitutionally apply its proscription of abortion as written to a woman in that stage of pregnancy. Nonetheless, the Court uses her complaint against the Texas statute as a fulcrum for deciding that States may impose virtually no restrictions on medical abortions performed during the first trimester of pregnancy. In deciding such a hypothetical lawsuit, the Court departs from the long-standing admonition that it should never "formulate a rule of constitutional law broader than is required by the precise facts to which it is to be applied."

The Right to Privacy Is Questioned

Even if there were a plaintiff in this case capable of litigating the issue which the Court decides, I would reach a conclusion opposite to that reached by the Court. I have difficulty in concluding, as the Court does, that the right of "privacy" is involved in this case. Texas, by the statute here challenged, bars the performance of a medical abortion by a licensed physician on a plaintiff such as Roe. A transaction resulting in an operation such as this is not "private" in the ordinary usage of that word. Nor is the "privacy" that the Court finds here even a distant relative of the freedom from searches and seizures protected by the Fourth Amendment to the Constitution, which the Court has referred to as embodying a right to privacy.

If the Court means by the term "privacy" no more than that the claim of a person to be free from unwanted state regulation of consensual transactions may be a form of "liberty" protected by the Fourteenth Amendment, there is no doubt that similar claims have been upheld in our earlier decisions on the basis of that liberty. I agree with the statement of Mr. Justice Stewart in his concurring opinion that the "liberty," against deprivation of which without due process the Fourteenth Amendment protects, embraces more than the rights found in the Bill of Rights. But that liberty is not guaranteed absolutely against deprivation, only against deprivation without due process of law. The test traditionally applied in the area of social and economic legislation is whether or not a law such as that challenged has a rational relation to a valid state objective. The Due Process Clause of the Fourteenth Amendment undoubtedly does place a limit, albeit a broad one, on legislative power to enact laws such as this. If the Texas statute were to prohibit an abortion even where the mother's life is in jeopardy, I have little doubt that such a statute would lack a rational relation to a valid state objective under the test stated in Williamson, supra. But the Court's sweeping invalidation of any restrictions on abortion during the first trimester is impossible to justify under that standard, and the conscious weighing of competing factors that the Court's opinion apparently substitutes for the established test is far more appropriate to a legislative judgment than to a judicial one.

The Right to Abortion Is Not Universally Accepted

The Court eschews the history of the Fourteenth Amendment in its reliance on the "compelling state interest" test. But the Court adds a new wrinkle to this test by transposing it from the legal considerations associated with the Equal Protection Clause of the Fourteenth Amendment to this case arising under the Due Process Clause of the Fourteenth Amendment. Unless I misapprehend the consequences of this transplanting of the "compelling state interest test," the Court's opinion will accomplish the seemingly impossible feat of leaving this area of the law more confused than it found it.

While the Court's opinion quotes from the dissent of Mr. Justice Holmes in *Lochner v. New York*, the result it reaches is more closely attuned to the majority opinion of Mr. Justice Peckham in that case. As in Lochner and similar cases applying substantive due process standards to economic and social welfare legislation, the adoption of the compelling state interest standard will inevitably require this Court to examine the legislative policies and pass on the wisdom of these policies in the very process of deciding whether a particular state interest put forward may or may not be "compelling." The decision here to break pregnancy into three distinct terms and to outline the permissible restrictions the State may impose in each one, for example, partakes more of judicial legislation than it does of a determination of the intent of the drafters of the Fourteenth Amendment.

The fact that a majority of the States reflecting, after all, the majority sentiment in those States, have had restrictions on abortions for at least a century is a strong indication, it seems to me, that the asserted right to an abortion is not "so rooted in the traditions and conscience of our people as to be ranked as fundamental." Even today, when society's views on abortion are changing, the very existence of the debate is evidence that the "right" to an abortion is not so universally accepted as the appellant would have us believe.

To reach its result, the Court necessarily has had to find within the scope of the Fourteenth Amendment a right that was apparently completely unknown to the drafters of the Amendment. As early as 1821, the first state law dealing directly with abortion was enacted by the Connecticut Legislature. By the time of the adoption of the Fourteenth Amendment in 1868, there were at least 36 laws enacted by state or territorial legislatures limiting abortion. While many States have amended or updated their laws, 21 of the laws on the books in 1868 remain in effect today. Indeed, the Texas statute struck down today was, as the majority notes, first enacted in 1857 and "has remained substantially unchanged to the present time."

There apparently was no question concerning the validity of this provision or of any of the other state statutes when the Fourteenth Amendment was adopted. The only conclusion possible from this history is that the drafters did not intend to have the Fourteenth Amendment withdraw from the States the power to legislate with respect to this matter.

The Texas Law Should Not Have Been Invalidated

Even if one were to agree that the case that the Court decides were here, and that the enunciation of the substantive constitutional law in the Court's opinion were proper, the actual disposition of the case by the Court is still difficult to justify. The Texas statute is struck down in toto, even though the Court apparently concedes that at later periods of pregnancy Texas might impose these selfsame statutory limitations on abortion. My understanding of past practice is that a statute found to be invalid as applied to a particular plaintiff, but not unconstitutional as a whole, is not simply "struck down" but is, instead, declared unconstitutional as applied to the fact situation before the Court.

For all of the foregoing reasons, I respectfully dissent.

The 1976 Hyde Amendment Harms Poor Women

Marie Cocco

Illinois representative Henry Hyde successfully sponsored legislation in 1976 that came to be known as the Hyde amendment. Under the law, abortion is no longer covered by Medicaid. In addition, health plans for federal employees, military personnel, and women in federal prisons exclude abortion coverage. In the following viewpoint Marie Cocco analyzes the Hyde amendment, which she sees as harmful to poor women, who must now resort to illegal abortions. Cocco writes for the Washington Post Writers Group.

R ep. Henry Hyde has announced his retirement, so it is an appropriate time to reconsider the Hypocrisy amendment.

Americans do not know the grandfather of all antiabortion legislation by that name. They know it as the Hyde amendment, a law on the books since 1976 that denies federal Medicaid funding for poor women who seek abortions. Though the prohibition applies only to federal money, the Hyde amendment has in practice meant that most states do not cover abortions using their Medicaid funds, either. Poor women who want an abortion—even for clear medical reasons—are denied them or are forced to scrounge up the money by scrimping on rent or food.

Those who beg or borrow the money wait far longer to have abortions than most other American women. Second-trimester abortions are common among the poor, even though the delay adds hundreds to the cost and can introduce harrowing medical complications.

Marie Cocco, "Rep. Henry Hyde," *Washington Post Writers Group,* April 2005. Copyright © 2005 by The Washington Post Writers Group. Reproduced by permission.

Immediate Repercussions

On his Web site, Hyde, 81, an Illinois Republican, cited among his proudest achievements in his congressional career "protecting the lives of the defenseless unborn." There was no mention of the tragedies his law has wrought upon those already born.

The first known victim of the Hyde amendment was Rosie Jimenez, a 27-year-old resident of Texas with a 5-year-old daughter and a freshly awarded $700 college scholarship. Finding herself pregnant, unable to obtain an abortion under Medicaid—and unwilling to give up her scholarship money, which she hoped was her daughter's ticket to a better life—Jimenez sought an illegal abortion and died of complications from it, weeks after the Hyde amendment took effect.

A 1979 study by the Centers for Disease Control and Prevention linked four deaths to the unavailability of Medicaid funding for abortions. More common than illegal abortions, though, are other desperate measures that desperate women take. Like the case of the rubbing alcohol. "I'll never forget that one," says Shawn Towey, who in the 1990s ran the Greater Philadelphia Women's Medical Fund, which helps poor women pay for abortions.

The 17-year-old girl from West Philadelphia already had one child when she became pregnant again. "It was a pretty sad story. Both her parents were in prison. She'd already had one kid who'd been taken away from her," recalls Towey, who now works for the National Network of Abortion Funds.

The teenager knew she couldn't obtain a Medicaid-funded abortion, nor afford one on her own. So she drank a bottle of rubbing alcohol, thinking it would cause a miscarriage. She wound up instead in an intensive-care burn unit of a Catholic hospital, where she vowed to try to abort again—no matter how self-destructive she had to be. No doctor would recommend an abortion under Pennsylvania's Medicaid law, which allows funding if the mother's life is in danger. A sympathetic nurse referred the teenager to the Greater Philadelphia Women's Medical Fund.

Amendment Is Hypocritical

The hypocrisy of the Hyde amendment is blatant, odious and long ignored, even by abortion-rights supporters who seem to have given up trying to rectify the injustice. Let us count the corruptions.

No medical procedure involving men on Medicaid—or any other form of insurance—is denied them because politicians find it objectionable. No other constitutional right is denied—by legislative fiat—because the citizen hasn't the money to exercise that right. No other policy that so obviously discriminates against minorities still is considered politically acceptable.

For years the very same politicians who voted to deny Medicaid abortion funding denounced poor women as irresponsible baby machines and welfare queens. The 1996 welfare revision enshrined the perfidy in federal law: Its "family cap" denies additional support to a woman who has another child while on welfare. No money for abortions; none for babies, either.

Hyde's casualties are disproportionately poor but they are no longer alone. Over the years, his amendment became the template for curtailing access to abortion for a range of women: federal employees who get health insurance through their jobs, women serving in the military and the Peace Corps, those served by the Indian Health Service and residents of the District of Columbia—all are denied coverage. The current movement to enact "conscience clauses" that would go so far as allowing pharmacists to refuse to fill prescriptions for ordinary birth-control pills has its philosophical roots in Hyde's amendment.

Retirement finally will cut Hyde's meddlesome reach. He'll be gone from women's lives but not forgotten. He's already done too much damage for that.

Planned Parenthood v. Casey Undermines Morality

Charles Colson

The 1992 case of Planned Parenthood v. Casey *challenged restrictions that the state of Pennsylvania had incorporated into its abortion laws, including informed consent, parental notification for minors, and record-keeping requirements, among others. The Supreme Court decision was considered a victory for both sides because it upheld the core of* Roe v. Wade, *which legalized abortion, yet it allowed individual states to impose "reasonable" restrictions on abortion. In the following viewpoint Charles Colson explores the potential ramifications of* Planned Parenthood v. Casey, *which in his opinion could include the sanctioning of euthanasia, homosexual sodomy, polygamy, adult incest, and suicide. Colson argues that by making virtually any kind of personal choice a right under the Fourteenth Amendment,* Casey *threatens to undermine public morality. Colson is chairman and founder of the Wilberforce Forum, a Christian social and political think tank. He is also the author of several books, including* Born Again *and* The Christian in Today's Culture.

Two years ago [in 1992] in this space I described a genial dinner party that ended on a sour note. A Christian friend shocked me by promoting abortion as a solution to ghetto poverty. At that time, I warned readers that just such sincere, well-meaning people would start us down a slippery slide into a culture of death. Little did I realize how quickly that slide would become a free fall. In a mere 24 months, an extraordinary shift has occurred that pushes us beyond abortion, beyond even the broader life issues, and into questions of whether we can maintain public order in a free society.

Charles Colson, "Casey Strikes Out," *Christianity Today,* October 3, 1994, p. 104. Copyright © 1994 by Charles Colson. Reproduced by permission.

The shift was precipitated dramatically and unexpectedly by the Supreme Court's 1992 ruling *Planned Parenthood v. Casey*. Initially, both sides felt it was a middle-of-the-road decision. Pro-lifers were glad that the Court allowed states to impose some reasonable limits on abortion; pro-choicers that the Court reaffirmed the basic holding of *Roe v. Wade*.

Casey Strengthened *Roe v. Wade*

But as the smoke cleared, it became obvious that the battle lines had shifted decisively. First, in *Roe* the Court had based abortion on the right to privacy, a right found nowhere explicitly in the Constitution—making the decision vulnerable to reversal. But in *Casey*, the Court transferred abortion from an implied to an explicit right—the right of liberty found in the Fourteenth Amendment—making the decision almost impossible to reverse.

Second, *Casey* opened the floodgates for euthanasia and other life-and-death issues. In pinning abortion to liberty, the Court defined *liberty* in the most sweeping terms conceivable—including, the majority said, "the most intimate and personal choices a person may make in a lifetime, choices central to personal dignity and autonomy."

[In May 1994,] U.S. District Judge Barbara Rothstein echoed that language when she struck down a Washington law prohibiting doctor-assisted suicide. Rothstein argued that suicide, like abortion, "involved the most intimate and personal choices a person may make," that it "constitutes a choice central to personal dignity and autonomy," and that it deserves the same "protection from unwarranted governmental interference."

Third, *Casey* set up personal autonomy as the rule in every area of life. In defining *liberty*, the majority waxed downright philosophical: "At the heart of liberty is the right to define one's own concept of existence, of meaning, of the universe, and of the mystery of human life."

Liberty Becomes Philosophical

At first sight, this passage may seem unremarkable. Beliefs about existence, meaning, and the mystery of human life are religious, and religious freedom is guaranteed by the First Amendment. What makes the passage revolutionary is that it applies religious language specifically to *abortion*. It gives religious status to a completely individualistic act: an act that presumes the right of one person to take the life of another for purely private reasons, without any public accountability. The Court endorsed a philosophy of the autonomous individual defining his or her own reality in complete isolation— even to the point of taking the life of another person.

But if autonomous, personal choices may not be circumscribed in any way by the state, the rule of law is impossible. In his dissenting opinion, Justice Scalia was prophetic: Under the Court's expansive definition, he warned, *liberty* could encompass "homosexual sodomy, polygamy, adult incest, and suicide."

But that list is altogether too short: The truth is that *liberty* could now encompass virtually any decision by which an individual expresses his sense of "selfhood," "meaning," and "existence."

Freedom of Conscience

As Christians, our response ought to be that all this talk about personal choices and meaning is irrelevant. Our courts and legal system are not concerned with private religious and metaphysical beliefs but with public justice. People of different beliefs—from Christians to atheists to New Agers—may disagree vehemently over the meaning of life; yet we can all agree on standards of public justice and order, just as we can all agree to stop when the traffic signal is red.

We may hold different religious and philosophical *reasons* for stopping at the signal—different convictions regarding the source of moral authority. Christians hold a distinctive ethic that is based on Scripture and uniquely empowered by the indwelling Holy Spirit. Yet, as citizens, we also contend for a public philosophy, justified by prudential arguments, aimed at promoting the public good.

The distinction between private belief and public philosophy is crucial if we are to maintain freedom of conscience and at the same time maintain public order. But it is precisely this distinction that *Casey* denied. I gave up any attempt to frame a public philosophy: it simply opted out of the discussion altogether and transferred the most fundamental decisions about life and death to the purely private realm. In the words of Russell Hittinger of Catholic University, *Casey* granted citizens "a private franchise over matters of life and death."

Yesterday that franchise covered abortion; today, assisted suicide; and tomorrow—who knows? The Court has given up any notion that private behavior should be constrained by the public good.

Casey has taken us far beyond the issue of abortion, or even the broader life issues. It has begun to unravel America's civil contract. It is only a short step from here to barbarism.

Conflicting Opinions on the Legacy of *Roe v. Wade*

Barbara Brotman

In 2003, on the thirtieth anniversary of the Supreme Court's Roe v. Wade *decision legalizing abortion, Barbara Brotman asked thirty women to share their views on how they feel about the law. While many championed* Roe, *claiming that the decision vastly improved women's lives, others criticized the decision as leading to a devaluation of human life. The wide range of opinions on* Roe *illustrates how contentious abortion remains in America. Barbara Brotman has been a reporter for the* Chicago Tribune *since 1978.*

The decision was so momentous that its legalese title has become instantly recognizable shorthand. When you are talking about *Roe vs. Wade*—or simply *Roe*—you are clearly talking about abortion. Thirty years ago today, the U.S. Supreme Court in the *Roe vs. Wade* decision made abortion legal throughout the nation. Jane Roe, a pseudonymous single, pregnant woman in Texas, had asked the court to declare her state's criminal abortion statutes unconstitutional. The Supreme Court did so, ruling that those laws violated the due process clause of the 14th Amendment, which protects the right of privacy from state action. Such privacy, the court said, includes a woman's right to terminate her pregnancy. The decision was hailed as a boon to women's freedom and health, and decried as a constitutionally flawed accessory to murder. In the last 30 years, *Roe vs. Wade* has been defended, attacked, debated and whittled at its edges. In the same time, abortion has become the second most commonly performed medical procedure among women, after Caesarean sections. And

Barbara Brotman, "Three Decades of Roe vs. Wade," *Chicago Tribune,* January 22, 2003, p. 1. Copyright © 2003 by Tribune Media Services, Inc. All rights reserved. Reproduced by permission.

though abortion numbers have decreased since peaking in 1990, controversy still surrounds *Roe vs. Wade* and divides not only the Supreme Court justices but many Americans.

Norma McCorvey, a.k.a. "Jane Roe," 55, founder of Roe No More Ministry, an anti-abortion speaker's bureau based in Dallas: "It was my test case that legalized abortion, but Jan. 22 [2003] isn't a celebration to me. I've since repudiated my stance on abortion and think *Roe v. Wade* should be overturned. I've worked in four abortion clinics, and I've seen firsthand what abortion does to women. Though I had never had an abortion—my child was carried to term and given up for adoption—abortion was the sun around which my life orbited. Now, I'm 100 percent devoted to Jesus and 100 percent pro-life. No exceptions. No compromise."

Sarah Weddington, 57, winning attorney, Roe vs. Wade: "I'll never forget how scared I was before the *Roe* oral argument. I felt the fate of women on my shoulders. On Jan. 21, women were seeking back-alley abortions, often ending up in emergency rooms. On the 22nd, abortion was legal, safe, and almost instantly available. The contrast was night and day. Now I worry about the future. The U.S. president, attorney general and Senate are lined up against *Roe*. Younger women must make this cause their own, to stop the path toward *Roe*'s destruction."

Kate McGowan, 41, of Clarendon Hills, director of marketing and communications for a software company: "I feel extremely strongly that it has to be legal. We should have the right to control our own reproductive organs. But as I've gotten older, I've gotten a lot more ambivalent. Mostly it's becoming a mom, and partly the maturity of being able to look at the other side. I look at my two kids; they started out as that tiny little bunch of cells that had a heartbeat. . . . But I would never presume that I can make the choice for someone else."

Sue Bergquist, 60, a Naperville anti-abortion activist who has been arrested numerous times outside abortion clinics and has adopted eight disabled children: "I was in the kitchen making dinner and I heard the decision on television. It's like the shooting of President Kennedy. Suddenly . . . our nation was not safe any more. We did not protect life. It was overwhelming to me. And it was a real wedge between me and my best friend, who had stood up in my wedding and I stood up in hers. She felt that a woman should have the right to do what she wanted with her own body. We had never discussed these things before. That was the parting of our ways. . . . God never makes mistakes. Just because [special needs children] have a disability doesn't mean they don't have a valuable life."

Pamela Robison, 20, of Gurnee, film student at Columbia College: "Half the people I know would have kids already [without *Roe*]. Thank God they don't. In a sense, it's been bad; there's less personal responsibility because you have that option. But overall, it's really important to have. When my mother was my age, she had two kids and a third on the way. I can't comprehend that. I have a career ahead of me."

Emily Lyons, 46, former nursing director of a Birmingham, Ala., women's clinic that was bombed on Jan. 29, 1998: "When the bomb, filled with dynamite and hundreds of roofing nails, exploded, it left a fist-size hole in my abdomen, took my eyelids, left eye, and parts of my intestines, tore the skin and muscles off my legs, and killed a police officer. Somebody tried to kill me because I worked at an abortion clinic. But it made me stubborn, determined, more outspoken. Freedom, like most things of value, has a very high price. I'm here to tell you it's worth it."

Kay Pankau, 44, of Elmhurst, a former lawyer and nurse now home with five children: "It's a personal decision that people have to make for themselves. But I have a hard time [with it].

It would be horribly sinful to abort a 9-month viable fetus. Where do you draw the line? We can save 26-week-old fetuses now. For myself, I wouldn't draw it. But for others, I wouldn't presume to know. I don't think this issue will ever go away. Our church asked us to refrain from voting for someone who would keep *Roe* legal. I did refrain. Would I do it again? I'm not sure."

Kelley Hoopis, 25, Chicago tax analyst: "I'm pro-life but do support emergency contraception and wish it were more readily available as it could assist in solving many unwanted pregnancies. I think abortions are overused by many—not all—young women, assuming it's a quick fix to an unwanted situation. Unfortunately, every action has an effect, positive or negative, and I believe the effects of an abortion are far more damaging than people realize."

Luz Alvarez Martinez, 60, executive director, National Latina Health Organization, based in Oakland: "The myth persists that Latinas don't believe in abortion or birth control. We do support the legality of abortion, but women need access to these and other reproductive health services. Abortions are currently only available in 14 percent of U.S. counties. There are issues of cost and parental consent. For Latinas, language and cultural barriers exist, some may lack proper documentation, and racial discrimination is still alive and well. So the term 'legal' is still not real for many women in this country."

Beth Haworth, 18, of Superior, Wis., president of Superior Teens for Life: "People my age need to know the truth. I think they know that abortion is legal, but I don't think they know exactly what it is and the severity of it. They don't realize that it's affected them, that they're missing one-third of their class. . . . It really has given us the free-sex idea for my peers. Now there are no consequences. If you get pregnant, just have an abortion and all your problems will be solved, or so the media would have you believe."

Kristin Sadie, 33, director of young adult ministry, Holy Name Cathedral: "I think this and many other factors shaped our generation. There is more talk, it seems to me, of private decisions [and less] of the role of the community in the life of a person. . . . The whole phrase 'personally opposed, but . . .' has been adopted for many different issues. There is a culture that other people really shouldn't have much influence on private morality. The debate has shifted as the years have passed from 'Is it a life?' to 'Whose decision is it?' I think the first question is an important one not to be neglected."

Anonymous, 34, City of Chicago health worker, had an abortion at age 26: "If abortion is outlawed, who will make up for women's missed education, increased cost of living, lack of parenting skills? What if you don't have the support of your family, you're a student, you're poor or lack health insurance? The decision isn't made in a vacuum—the ramifications are immense—and the law has to account for that."

Lorraine Cole, 52, president, National Black Women's Health Project in Washington, D.C.: "Too often for poor women, decisions about reproduction are not a matter of choice, but the result of an absence of choices. Welfare policies that deny certain benefits can pressure poor women to take irreversible measures to prevent pregnancy or to decide to terminate an unplanned pregnancy. Also, limitations on medical coverage for reproductive health services for poor women deny the right to choose from the full range of reproductive health options."

Emily, 26, sales associate, New Hampshire, had an abortion at age 19: "I don't see how anybody can give advice on this topic, period. If it's not your body, it's not your decision. It was probably the most horrible thing I've ever gone through emotionally, but I'm glad it was my decision. I have to live with it and it's tough. Just because it was my decision to make doesn't mean I took it lightly."

Rabbi Ellen W. Dreyfus, 50, president, Chicago Board of Rabbis: "The reason *Roe v. Wade* is so important, is that the decision whether or not to have an abortion should be a medical and religious decision and not a political one. I don't want state legislators in my bedroom or my [doctor's] office when I or other women are making decisions about our reproductive health. Judaism would say this is a difficult decision that should be made by a woman in consultation with her partner, her doctor, her rabbi and her God."

Bernadette Borgard, 43, of Downers Grove, adoptive mother of three: "The birth mother of my oldest daughter went into one of those clinics, in Florida, that supposedly is an abortion clinic, but isn't. She was shown graphic images of abortion. She ran out of there crying. She gave birth to Hannah and we adopted her. . . . I've always been against abortion. I feel very sad for women who feel they have to get an abortion. But if you sleep with somebody, you could get pregnant. That's a life. But I don't like the alternative, either. I don't like women having botched abortions. I don't know what the answer is."

Dr. Sadja Greenwood, 72, a retired physician who had an illegal abortion in college and in 1973 was running a teen clinic in San Francisco for Planned Parenthood: "When I got to medical school, I saw women who came into the emergency room having done things like put potassium permanganate in their vagina to stimulate bleeding. It also eroded a hole in the wall between the vagina and rectum. I saw people who put soap suds solutions in there, who had their cervix penetrated with knitting needles. It was just horrifying. And they were treated like criminals. It's not a question of having abortions or not having abortions. It's, are they going to be legal, are they going to be safe? We just can't go back to that nightmare."

Elaine Bellis, 59, archdeacon of the Episcopal Diocese of Chicago: "I believe a woman does have a choice, but as a minister,

I would not counsel her to have an abortion. My feeling is Jesus came to save life, not take lives. But he also gave us free will. If it's a matter of saving her life, or a sexual assault, I would say, 'Be thoughtful about it. Other options exist.' If abortion was her decision, I would support her."

Dr. Nehama Dresner, 42, assistant professor of psychiatry and obstetrics and gynecology, Northwestern University Medical School: "Across all socioeconomic, cultural and religious backgrounds, women struggle with reproductive decisions. Studies clearly show that women denied reproductive choice are at greater risk for psychiatric symptoms and illness than those able to follow through on a decision to terminate, as painful as that may be. Children born to mothers who sought termination and were denied are at higher risk for psychiatric and behavioral disorders. Reproductive choice is an essential freedom that holds tremendous responsibility and moves us closer to planned, desired, healthy pregnancies for women."

Vicki Thorn, 53, executive director, National Office of Post Abortion Reconciliation and Healing, in Milwaukee: "I'm amazed by the universality of the reactions of women who have had abortions. The regret, the grief, the what-might-have-beens. Men and other family members are equally impacted. Women need to know that if they've had an abortion and need help, its available. Also, women need to get serious about demanding research on abortion's long-term health implications. . . . We need to ask, 'Is abortion good medicine for women?'"

Kate Michelman, 60, president of NARAL: Pro-choice America (formerly the National Abortion and Reproductive Rights Action League): "I experienced the humiliation of not being recognized as a person able to make my own decision about pregnancy and childbearing when, in 1970, I had my choice of a back-alley abortion or suffering the indignities of being deemed unfit for motherhood by a hospital panel, (which was one way a woman could obtain a therapeutic abortion before *Roe*). Being forced to consider risking my life to make a responsible decision for my family profoundly changed me. *Roe* said women will be the moral arbiters of their lives. It's not about abortion, it's about the essence of who we are as women."

Deborah Erdmann, 36, of Palatine, homemaker and physical therapist: "I remember in high school thinking, 'Oh, its a woman's body, its just a blob of tissue, she should be able to do what she wants.' But my family was very strongly pro-life. I thought, I should look into this. And as I looked into the science of it, I realized, 'This is an entirely separate life.' One of government's primary responsibilities is to stand up for those who can't stand up for themselves. The media vilify pro-lifers as just caring about the baby before it's born, not the mother or child. But we have supported agencies for years that give to young teen mothers."

Joanne Falco, 65, of Mt. Prospect, mother of two grown children: "The United States Supreme Court has replaced the God of Abraham, Isaac and Jacob. The courts have ignored God's laws, and our society stands and applauds the new god—the god of self-centeredness, selfishness, self-gratification, self-esteem, 'tolerance.' The deep maternal instinct that is planted in a woman's heart to protect and nurture the child is also killed (by abortion), and the rights of the father are not considered. The approval of the court's ruling on *Roe v. Wade* has played a major role in bringing about the death of our nation's conscience. God is not mocked. What we sow, we reap."

Lynn Kahn, 60, former assistant director of counseling for the Hope Clinic for Women in Granite City, Ill.: "At 24, I was raped and became pregnant. When a friend told me about abortion, I didn't even think about the dangers—I just knew I had something alien inside me. A woman came, inserted a tube inside me and left me overnight. At the hospital, bleeding and infected, I begged the doctor not to call the police. But even frightened and in pain, I did not regret my decision."

Mary Anne Hackett, president of the Illinois Right to Life Committee: "I remember reading it in the paper in the morning. I remember sitting down and crying. . . . At high schools, it's been legal as long as [the students have] been alive. Students wonder why I'm all wrought-up. But it's because it's such a damaging thing to our whole country. It's damaging to women. It's been damaging to families. I feel sorry for the young girls. They're afraid, and want a quick fix. Then they have to bear the consequences."

Naomi Wolf, 40, author and feminist: "Nothing that I or that any of my generation value and take for granted—jobs, families, choices, education, hopes, sense of identity—could have been possible without *Roe v. Wade.* . . . We should now strive for an America in which there are very few abortions because women and men act responsibly in sexual settings and, if birth control fails, there is a vast network of support. The fact that so many pregnancies in America end in abortion is not a sign of our freedom. It is a sign that women do not have the choices and autonomy yet . . . that they need."

Kari Skloot, 37, of Buffalo Grove, executive director of the Illinois chapter of Resolve: The National Infertility Association, who underwent eight years of infertility treatments before adopting a son: "We were the beneficiaries of a woman's reproductive decision; we were fortunate that she chose us to parent her child. My feelings remain solid that women should have that right to make those decisions. The fact that I was not able to conceive and carry a child didn't change my feelings about that at all. I don't find it a conflict; I kind of feel that its two sides of the same coin."

Dr. Junda Woo, 35, Houston, first recipient of the Barnett A. Slepian Memorial Fund in 2000, named after the obstetrician/ gynecologist shot and killed in his home on Oct. 23, 1998, by an anti-abortion activist: "I think people believe that providing abortions is depressing, but its incredibly rewarding. This is one of few areas where you can intervene at a crisis moment in a woman's life and help turn everything around. Things like the Texas Supreme Court's recent decision that the state need not fund abortions for poor, seriously ill women—or the fact that 93 percent of Texas counties have no abortion provider—strengthen my resolve to provide abortions."

Wanda Franz, 59, president, National Right to Life Committee: "I think it has coarsened American life. It has introduced an element of violence, of the ability to legally take the life of another person if they're inconvenient to you. . . . I don't see how this is an advance for women. It is a huge step backward to where women are being used again as sexual objects and discarded when they're done with them, particularly when they're 'polluted' with the presence of a child."

Liz Waits, 22, senior at Wheaton College; Waits is ranked ninth out of all 1,500 ROTC graduates in 2003 nationwide, and first among women: "I think for my generation, it's kind of become a way of life. For me, it's like studying history. . . . I am personally pro-life. With my female friends, it causes kind of a rift between those who are pro-choice and those who are pro-life. I think a lot of that has been caused by pro-lifers themselves. I personally feel there's been way too much emphasis placed on, 'Is this a person or a fetus?' and a lot less on the women themselves. It's important to really sympathize with these women and let them know we realize abortion is not the easy way out."

Antiabortion Legislation Is Gaining Ground

Jodi Enda

In this selection Jodi Enda explores the evolution of abortion laws since Roe v. Wade *legalized abortion in 1973. Enda explains that states have passed 409 new laws restricting abortion in the last decade alone. According to her, abortion proponents are losing the battle to those who want to make the procedure illegal. Americans are increasingly concerned about the moral status of the fetus, she points out, resulting in less support for abortion. Enda is a journalist who covers politics and government. She previously reported on the White House, presidential elections, and Congress for Knight Ridder newspapers.*

Kimberly was at home with her two sleeping children when her estranged husband, high on methamphetamines and angry about their impending divorce, showed up at her door last September [2004].

"He came in and said he wanted to talk about child-support payments. We were fighting about everything. The divorce was not final," Kimberly said. "He raped me."

Kimberly didn't call the police because she wanted to protect her children from further trauma. Their lives had been upended during the previous two and a half years, ever since she was pregnant with her younger son and discovered that her husband was an addict. Since then, he'd quit his job, and she'd worked two; he put $50,000 on their credit cards at casinos and strip clubs; he threatened to kill her when she moved out with the boys; and he stole $700 from her boss, costing her a part-time bookkeeping job. After taking medical leave

Jodi Enda, "The Women's View," *The American Prospect*, April 2005, pp. 22–27. Copyright © 2005 by The American Prospect, Inc. All rights reserved. Reproduced by permission of *The American Prospect*, 11 Beacon St., Suite 1120, Boston, MA 02108.

because she feared a nervous breakdown, Kimberly was fired from her primary job in the business department of a Phoenix TV station.

Pregnant and Desperate

Kimberly, then 33, didn't tell anyone about the rape, not even her closest friends. "I had no strength," she explained. Two weeks later, she realized she was pregnant. She didn't tell anyone about that, either.

She wanted an abortion, but she couldn't afford one. "I didn't know what to do," she said. "There was no way I could have had that baby. My ex would have killed me. That was never an option." Adoption wasn't, either. Kimberly couldn't bring herself to let her pregnancy show in Phoenix, and she couldn't leave town for several months the way women used to when they got pregnant out of wedlock. "I couldn't take my kids, and I couldn't leave them with my ex. I couldn't bring another child into this world. It came out of this . . . ," she said, swallowing the word "rape" as she uttered it.

So, Kimberly thought, she'd wait until she could scrape together enough money for an abortion. She had no idea how difficult that would be. "I didn't realize that the price was going up and up and up each week [as] I was going further along."

Desperate and without medical care, Kimberly went to the state for help. She qualified for Medicaid, but was told it wouldn't cover her abortion. She found a Web site that showed her how to apply to nonprofit groups for money to pay for an abortion. The Minneapolis-based Hersey Abortion Assistance Fund offered her $100, not nearly enough. Determined not to let the fetus reach the point of viability (generally interpreted to be 24 weeks gestation in Arizona), after which the state prohibits most abortions, Kimberly applied to dozens of funds around the country and sold her TV. By the end of January, she'd pulled together $900, the amount one clinic had told her was enough to cover her second-trimester abortion. She made an appointment for the two-day procedure.

When she went in the first day, the sonogram showed that she was nearly 20 weeks into her pregnancy. The abortion would cost $1,000. She didn't have it. The doctor said Kimberly would have to get the money by the next morning or postpone the procedure another week, which would drive up the price again. She sat in a park and cried.

By the next morning, Kimberly had managed to get another $100 from an abortion fund, but the delay made her miss the training session for her brand-new state job. She lost the job.

The Larger Abortion Debate

As I listened to Kimberly pour out her story just three weeks after her abortion, I was struck not only by the tragedy of her situation, the rawness of her emotions, but by what it meant to the larger abortion debate. Here was a mother who was struggling to take care of a 5-year-old and a 2-year-old in the face of incredible psychological and financial hardships, a woman striving to make a moral decision for her family. She did not want an abortion. She didn't even want the sex that led to her pregnancy. But having had the latter forced on her, she felt the former was the best response.

Decades ago, supporters of abortion rights used women like Kimberly to illustrate a need and a danger. The male doctors and clergy members who were at the forefront of the modern abortion-rights movement argued that the procedure was necessary to protect women from death or injury brought on by botched, illegal abortions. Feminists asserted that women must have control over their own lives.

The movement won a tremendous victory on January 22, 1973, when the Supreme Court handed down *Roe v. Wade* and legalized abortion. Since then, abortion opponents have worked methodically, state by state, to chip away at what they saw as nearly unfettered access to abortion. Now, that access is very fettered indeed. State legislatures have passed more than 400 laws limiting access to abortion in the past decade alone. According to the Alan Guttmacher Institute, a pro-choice think tank whose statistics are cited by both sides, abortion is available in only 13 percent of U.S. counties.

A Brilliant Public-Relations Campaign

Nationally, President George W. Bush in 2003 signed the first federal law—since blocked by three courts in rulings the administration is appealing—that would criminalize one or more abortion procedures. And in his second term, this most anti-abortion of presidents is almost certain to appoint some justices to the Supreme Court, potentially enough to reverse or further weaken *Roe*. (Pro-choice leaders estimate that if *Roe* were overturned, 30 states would immediately outlaw abortion except in extreme circumstances.) Meanwhile, the Republican Congress is bent on passing additional legislation to restrict access to abortion or, like the Partial-Birth Abortion Ban Act of 2003, to reduce public support for it simply by making people queasy.

Abortion opponents have engaged in a brilliant public-relations campaign designed to manipulate the emotions of a nation that overwhelmingly supports abortion rights, but with some limits. They've used issues like "partial-birth abortion," a term they made up, to play to a general uneasiness, a discomfort felt not only by abortion opponents but by some pro-choicers as well. They've made us nervous about the "unborn," and in doing so obscured the concern we used to feel for women in dire situations.

While the right has appealed to our sentiments, the left has relied on dry legal arguments, abandoning the 1960s-style speak-outs that so successfully demonstrated why women like Kimberly need choices. But today those sorts of arguments are critical: We've just moved into an era when every woman of childbearing age has always had the right to choose abortion. Young women don't remember the hangers and back alleys; they didn't live with the fear. And now, when a right they've taken for granted is in jeopardy, virtually the only people speaking out about their choice to terminate a pregnancy are those who say they regret having made it. . . .

Humanizing Fetuses

The opposition has done a lot to humanize fetuses. The emotional appeal against abortion reached its pinnacle in the last 10 years, when anti-abortion forces served up a genius campaign against what they dubbed "partial-birth abortion," a graphic term that doesn't exist in medical textbooks. Pro-choice leaders, ill-prepared to wrangle in human, as opposed to legal, terms, appeared to be twiddling their thumbs. Though not one abortion has been blocked by the ban, the gruesome images that accompanied the debate in Congress convinced even many abortion-rights supporters that this thing called "partial birth" was wrong.

Technology, too, has lent a hand to those who would end abortions. New 3D and 4D sonograms show in vivid detail what fetuses look like. How, some ask, can you abort a fetus after you've watched it suck its thumb?

Abortion battlers have proposed the Unborn Child Pain Awareness Act, which would require that providers inform women that fetuses can feel pain after 20 weeks gestation, and to offer them fetal anesthesia. (Tellingly, they don't offer money so that poor women could afford to spare their fetuses this trauma.) Pro-choice groups have been left standing on the side again.

Now, anti-abortion leaders are ratcheting up their emotional campaign further. Having raised sympathy for fetuses, they recently reached into the feminists' quiver to talk about what's best for women. Serrin Foster, president of Feminists for Life, contends that society has failed women by forcing them to choose between school or work and children. "We believe," she told me, "that abortion is a reflection that we have not met the needs of women."

Anti-Abortion Laws Are Increasing

Abortion opponents haven't won yet—*Roe* is still in place—but they can take solace in numbers. Abortion rates have fallen, in part because of better birth control, but also because of state laws. "Roe at this point has been so eviscerated that in many respects, although I don't want to see it overturned—heavens, no—the fact is that this current Supreme Court has thus far found almost no burden undue," said Gloria Feldt, who recently resigned as president of the Planned Parenthood Federation of America.

According to NARAL,[1] states enacted 409 anti-abortion laws in the past decade, 29 in 2004. NARAL reports that 47 states plus the District of Columbia allow individuals or institutions to refuse to provide women with abortions or other reproductive health services and referrals; 44 states require young women to notify or obtain consent from a parent before having an abortion, though 10 of the laws have been ruled unconstitutional; 33 states plus the District of Columbia ban public financing of abortions; 30 states have mandatory waiting periods of up to three days or requirements that abortion providers give women seeking abortions negative literature or lectures; 26 states restrict the performance of abortions to hospitals or specialized facilities; and 17 states prohibit insurance from covering abortions or require women to pay higher premiums for abortion care.

NOW's [National Organization for Women president Kim] Gandy said that even pro-choice lawmakers mistakenly fall victim to arguments that restrictions don't hurt women. "Unfortunately, the legislators on our side don't get it," she told

1. National Association for Repeal of Abortion Laws, now called NARAL Pro-Choice America

me. "They vote for these, what they call 'little restrictions,' all the time. It seems little to them, but the cumulative effect, or the effect on individual groups of women, can be enormous."

Abortion Rates Are Declining

As a result of restrictive laws, violence, and the stigma that has become attached to abortion, fewer doctors and other health-care professionals are providing them. The number of abortion providers declined from a high of 2,908 in 1982 to 1,819 in 2000, a 37-percent drop, according to the Guttmacher Institute. Almost no nonmetropolitan area had an abortion provider in 2000, the institute reported, which might explain why the abortion rate among women in small towns and rural areas is half that of women in metropolitan areas.

State restrictions almost certainly have caused some women, perhaps thousands a year, to forgo abortions. Research suggests that Wisconsin's two-day waiting period might have contributed to a 21-percent decline in abortions there. Shawn Towey, spokeswoman for the National Network of Abortion Funds, a group comprising 102 organizations that provides money and support for low-income women seeking abortions, estimates that 60,000 women a year find the restrictions so onerous that they carry their babies to term. The Guttmacher Institute stated in a 2001 report that between 18 percent and 35 percent of Medicaid-eligible women who want to have abortions continue their pregnancies if public funding isn't available.

"The biggest chunk of women who are unable to get abortions right now are poor women on Medicaid," said Towey. While 17 states do pay for the abortions of low-income women, 33 do not. "The big irony," she said, "is that low-income women get later abortions because they have to delay to save the money." The Guttmacher report said that 22 percent of Medicaid-eligible women who had second-trimester abortions would have ended their pregnancies earlier if the government paid.

And behind every one of these numbers lies the story of a woman.

Finding Common Ground

The good news, if there is any, is that women's rights activists are waking up to their public-relations problem. "I think we have to face the reality that public support for abortion is eroding," said Martha Burk, chair of the National Council of Women's Organizations. "I think we've clearly lost the terminology war. They keep coming up with very reasonable-sounding restrictions, and we are unable to counter that. . . . The movement is in a bind."

Feldt said, "For way too many years, the pro-choice movement was reacting to things. They thought they had won, and when you win you only have to defend. When you are in a defensive posture, your adversaries will nibble off one finger at a time, and pretty soon your whole arm is gone." That's precisely what happened when Congress passed the 2003 abortion ban, Feldt said.

"The ban . . . was not our finest moment," Kate Michelman of NARAL agreed. "We got caught up on numbers and procedures and we allowed the other side to define the terrain." . . .

The choice itself—the opportunity to decide—is essential to women's lives. Burk put it like this: "It's not just about whether and when to have children. It's about timing. It's about being able to be free of abusive relationships . . . the ability to go ahead with a career. . . . It's about how your life unfolds. It can mean the difference in being dependent on government largesse or not for great periods of your life. It can mean the difference in the quality of life for your other children." It can mean, she said, not having a baby at the age of 12. It can mean surviving.

But when politicians and lobbyists argue, it's rarely about 12-year-old girls. More likely, it's about 12-week-old fetuses.

It's time to turn the conversation back—back to women, back to children, back to people who have been born. Frances Kissling, president of Catholics for a Free Choice, said this might mean acknowledging the growing connection Americans have to fetuses, and the moral complexity behind abortion. Pro-choice leaders need to talk about abortion the way women talk about it at their kitchen tables, Kissling asserted. "My experience with women at abortion clinics is they largely understand the nuances of what's going on," she said. "They do not come in waving the flag and pounding their shoe on the table demanding an abortion as a political right. They come in . . . as rich human beings dealing with a conflict of values. They come in fully aware that the life that is developing within them has value. To me that doesn't give it rights, that doesn't make it a person. Its developing humanity still comes into conflict with women's lives and aspirations."

It's that sense of the fetus that's convinced some in the pro-choice movement that they should stand back during the upcoming congressional debate on the "fetal pain" bill[2] which wouldn't restrict abortion, but which would continue to humanize fetuses.

The challenge for pro-choicers is to balance America's growing sympathy for fetuses with an equal- or greater-concern for women. They must counter the image of a humanized fetus with that of a human, caring, and sometimes suffering woman—with a woman who has needs and feelings and morals. The argument won't win over staunch abortion foes. But it should strike a chord with mainstream Americans, the very people the abortion-rights movement needs to reach. The pro-choice movement must speak the language of real people—and maybe even let real people, like Kimberly, speak.

2. This bill is in the first step of the legislative process. It was referred to the Senate Committee on Health, Education, Labor, and Pensions in January 2005.

CHAPTER 2

Morality and Abortion

Chapter Preface

People on both sides of the abortion debate defend their positions using moral reasoning. For example, many people opposed to abortion point to religious teachings to argue that all human life is sacred from the point of conception. According to them, God created human life; thus fetuses must be revered as God's creations. On the other hand, those who support abortion claim that society has a moral obligation to protect human rights, including women's reproductive rights. They contend that women have a far greater moral claim on society than do fetuses, which are merely clusters of cells.

Ironically, at the center of these moral claims are scientific facts. For instance, abortion opponents bolster their argument that life begins at conception with the finding that embryos contain a complete set of DNA. Abortion critics interpret that fact as indicating that the fetus is a person, deserving of the protection granted to adult humans. Conversely, abortion proponents point to findings that the fetus does not possess the capacity to think as support for the argument that it is not a person. If the fetus is not a person, they reason, it does not deserve the protection afforded to adults.

The use of science to back up moral positions has been a relatively recent phenomenon. Whereas ethicists in the past might have relied entirely on religious teachings to support their claims, more recent thinkers are inclined to cite scientific facts to support their arguments. The trend makes sense considering how much confidence modern people have in scientists and the scientific method. It is no surprise, then, that as scientists have gained increasing knowledge about how human life begins, activists on both sides of the abortion debate would use their findings to win support for their respective positions.

Whether science will ever settle the abortion debate, however, is questionable. While the moral debate over abortion is often couched in scientific terms, the scientific facts at the center of the controversy will continue to be interpreted through the moral lenses of the people engaged in the debate. Thus it is likely that controversy over the morality of abortion will continue well into the future.

Abortion and Morality Throughout History

Alexander Sanger

Reproductive freedom is not a modern concept, according to Alexander Sanger. In the following selection Sanger explores the history of abortion in early times, and observes that reproductive freedom has been permitted throughout most of Western history. He explains that contraception and abortion were practiced as early as 1850 B.C., and both were considered legal and morally acceptable. The Christian Church did consider abortion sinful after quickening—the point at which a mother can feel the developing fetus—but it viewed abortion performed before that time as moral. Sanger is the grandson of birth control pioneer Margaret Sanger. He is the chairperson of the International Planned Parenthood Council.

The concept of reproductive freedom has been recognized to some extent throughout human history. Greek and Roman secular law and Jewish and Christian theology all recognized that there were times and circumstances where birth control and abortion were acceptable. At the time when the United States was founded, under English law, birth control and abortion were mostly legal, acceptable, and used.

My grandmother, Margaret Sanger, did not invent birth control. Contraceptive information appears in the earliest human writings. An Egyptian papyrus from about the year 1850 BCE contains a recipe for a vaginal suppository (of uncertain effectiveness and questionable hygiene since its main ingredient appears to be crocodile dung) to prevent pregnancy. Greek and Roman medical literature is rife with instructions for

Alexander Sanger, *Beyond Choice: Reproductive Freedom in the 21st Century.* New York: PublicAffairs, 2004. Copyright © 2004 by Alexander Sanger. All rights reserved. Reproduced by permission of PublicAffairs, a member of Perseus Books, L.L.C.

herbal methods of contraception and abortion (the French so-called abortion pill, RU-486 or mifepristone, is not a new concept). Greek and Roman law did not mention contraception but did regulate abortion as a matter of property law, requiring a husband's consent before his wife could have an abortion, since the fetus was considered the husband's personal property. Reproduction was a matter not only for the secular authorities in the Roman Empire; it was a matter for the new Christian Church as well.

Christianity and Reproduction

The Christian Church brought quite a different perspective to reproductive matters than the Roman Empire did. As a persecuted religious sect and eager for defensive and theological reasons to increase the number of Christians both by birth and conversion, the early Church was firmly pro-natalist. The main problem that early Christian theologians faced was that neither contraception nor abortion was specifically mentioned in the Bible, except for Exodus 21:22 which addressed the penalties to be imposed when a person causes an accidental miscarriage. The penalties were levied under the same theory manifested in Roman law. Penalties were merited because the father had been deprived of his property. Traditional Jewish teachings favored childbearing in order to have the Jewish race continue, but these teachings permitted, and in some cases even required, that birth control and abortion be used. Christian doctrine, which slowly emerged over the centuries after the New Testament was written, declared both contraception and abortion to be mostly, but not always, sinful. Christian theology took a more severe tone on reproductive issues after the Black Death decimated Christian Europe in the mid–fourteenth century. Many historians believe that the Church launched the witch hunts and the attendant Inquisition to prevent midwives, who were the leading purveyors of birth control and abortion methods to the women of Europe, from plying their trade.

The Church was not, however, entirely anti-abortion. For centuries, using the current state of scientific knowledge, the Church debated when a fetus became "human" and thus came under the protection of Church law against abortion. Plato and Aristotle had opined that the fetus wasn't "formed" or human until forty days after conception for the male and eighty days after conception for the female. Although easily dismissed as a sexist joke today, this theory was based on the biological knowledge of the time, in which every fetus was believed to have begun as male, and the female fetus was believed to be an in utero mutation from the male. At any rate, this belief was adopted by Christian theologians in later centuries and became the doctrine of delayed ensoulment, that is, the time when the soul entered the fetus and thus the fetus became "formed" or "human." The time of ensoulment was moved forward in time by Christian theologians from the Platonic fortieth or eightieth day to the time when the woman first felt the fetus move, usually during the fourth or fifth month of pregnancy. Thus, the humanness of an unborn child coincided with the time a woman could first confirm she was pregnant. Before this time, under early Christian doctrine, there was no "human being," and abortion during this period was not a sin. Under this doctrine, the moral status of an early fetus was less than that of a more developed fetus.

Secular Law

Secular law eventually adopted this theological concept of delaying the declaration of a pregnancy and thus of human life until the woman could confirm she was pregnant. In the Middle Ages English law, based on the notion of delayed ensoulment, defined pregnancy to begin at "quickening," the time when the pregnant woman first felt the fetus move. Before quickening, termination of the "pregnancy" was not prohibited because the woman was not deemed under the law to be pregnant. Legal historians today are divided on whether abortion even after quickening was considered a crime. Justice Harry Blackmun said in *Roe v. Wade* : "it now appears doubtful that abortion was ever firmly established as a common-law crime even with respect to the destruction of a quick fetus."

The use of quickening to determine the beginning of a pregnancy made sense in terms of two other biological facts that were probably unknown to theologians and lawmakers of the time. First, a substantial percentage of fertilized ova never implant in the uterus and hence a pregnancy never starts. One study showed that 58 percent of fertilized eggs did not survive until the twelfth day after conception. Second, there is a substantial risk of miscarriage in the early months of pregnancy even after implantation, a risk estimated to be between 10 or 20 percent of pregnancies, or perhaps more, since many early pregnancies are undetected and unreported. Taken together, this means, as biologist Lee M. Silver of Princeton University has stated, that 75 percent of fertilized eggs do not survive the nine months of pregnancy. The concept of declaring a pregnancy officially beginning at quickening, at the fourth or fifth months, recognized the biological uncertainties of early pregnancy. This concept has a lingering effect on American public opinion on abortion. Americans overwhelmingly approve of abortion being legal in the first trimester, that is, before quickening, and disapprove of abortion thereafter.

Abortion Issue Becomes Contentious

English law was carried over into American law in 1776 when we declared our independence and in 1789 when we formed our new nation. In both colonial and post-revolutionary America, abortion was legal at least up to the point of quickening, and perhaps thereafter. Contraception was not forbidden in either English or American law. Although much contraceptive knowledge was lost due to the witch hunts in

Europe beginning in the fifteenth century, in late eighteenth century America there were herbal methods for both contraception and abortion that were handed down from midwife to midwife and from mother to daughter. This is not to say that abortion was not a contentious issue in the colonies. In 1729 Benjamin Franklin was starting his career as a newspaper publisher and used the abortion issue to attack a rival publisher, Samuel Keimer. Keimer's paper thought it was providing a public service, or at least filling up its newspages, with entries from the encyclopedia. He started with the letter "a" and soon published the entry on abortion. Franklin, using the pen names Martha Careful and Celia Shortface, penned letters to another rival paper "feigning shock and indignation at Keimer's offense," as his biographer, Walter Isaacson, put it. Isaacson continued:

> As Miss Careful threatened, "If he proceeds farther to expose the secrets of our sex in that audacious manner (women would) run the hazard of taking him by the beard in the next place we meet him." Thus Franklin manufactured the first recorded abortion debate in America, not because he had any strong feelings on the issue, but because he knew it would help sell newspapers.

Throughout most of Western history, therefore, reproductive freedom, despite being a contentious issue, was permitted to a greater or lesser extent. Reproductive policy and law were the products of 1) the contemporary and limited understanding of reproductive biology; 2) the Christian Church's institutional need to increase the number of Christians (especially after the Black Death); and 3) the intertwining of Church and State which resulted in theological ensoulment being transformed into legal quickening.

Men Must Take Responsibility for Preventing Abortion

Susan B. Anthony

Early in life Susan B. Anthony developed a sense of justice and moral zeal that eventually led to her working on behalf of women's rights. In the following selection from her newspaper the Revolution, *Anthony reveals her adamant opposition to abortion—she refuses to even use the word, instead referring to it as "destroying the little being before it lives." Although Anthony claims that the woman who aborts her child is guilty of murder, she also asserts that the greater immorality lies with the man who does not take responsibility for unwanted pregnancies. She concludes that women should not be submissive, and men should respect women, which would result in better marriages that only produce children who are wanted and loved.*

In a late *Revolution* is an extract from the New York *Medical Gazette* rebuking a practice common among married women, and demanding a law for its suppression.

Much as I deplore the horrible crime of child-murder, earnestly as I desire its suppression, I cannot believe with the writer of the above-mentioned article, that such a law would have the desired effect. It seems to me to be only mowing off the top of the noxious weed, while the root remains.

We want *prevention*, not merely punishment. We must reach the *root* of the evil, and destroy it.

To my certain knowledge this crime is not confined to those whose love of ease, amusement and fashionable life leads them to desire immunity from the cares of children; but is practiced by those whose inmost souls revolt from the dreadful deed, and in whose hearts the maternal feeling is

Susan B. Anthony, "Marriage and Maternity," *The Revolution*, July 8, 1869, p. 4.

pure and undying. What then, has driven these women to the desperation necessary to force them to commit such a deed? This question being answered, I believe we shall have such an insight into the matter as to be able to talk more clearly of a remedy.

Rights Are Transferred to Husbands

Women are educated to think that with marriage their individuality ceases or is transferred to their husbands. The wife has thenceforth no right over her own body. This is also the husband's belief, and upon which he acts. No matter what her condition, physical or mental, no matter how ill-prepared she may feel herself for maternity, the demands of his passion must never be refused.

He thinks, or cares nothing, for the possible result of his gratification. If it be that an immortal being, with all its needs, physical, mental and moral, shall come into the world to sin, to suffer, to die, because of his few moments of pleasure, what cares he?

He says he is ready to provide for his children, therefore he feels himself a kind father, worthy of honor and love. That is, he is ready to provide for them food and clothing, but he is not willing to provide for them, by his self-denial, sound bodies, good tempers and a happy ante-natal existence. He gives his wife wealth, leisure and luxury, and is, therefore, a devoted husband, and she is an *undutiful*, unloving wife, if her feelings fail to respond to his.

Devoted husband! Devoted to what? To self-gratification at the expense of the respect of his wife. I know men who call themselves Christians, who would insist that they are *gentlemen*, who never insult any woman—but their wives. They think it impossible that they can outrage them; they never think that even in wedlock there may be the very vilest prostitution; and if Christian women are *prostitutes* to Christian husbands, what can we expect but the natural sequence—infanticide?

Women who are in the last stages of consumption, who know that their offspring must be puny, suffering, neglected orphans, are still compelled to submit to maternity, and dying in childbirth, are their husbands ever condemned? Oh, no! It was only his right as a husband he claimed, and if maternity or death ensued, surely he could not be blamed for that. He did not desire it. The usual tenor of men's conduct in this respect seems on a par with that of Henry VIII, who when asked if the life of his wife or of his child should be saved, as it seemed needful that one should be sacrificed, answered, "O the child, by all means. Wives are easily obtained."

Women Are Driven to Abortion

Women whose husbands are habitual drunkards and whose children are therefore idiotic, deformed creatures, and who feel assured that such must be the case with all their offspring, must yet submit. And if such a woman as the dying consumptive, rather than bring into the world such miserable children, rather perhaps than give life to a daughter to suffer all that she has endured, destroys the little being, as she thinks, before it lives, she would be punished by the law, and he, *the real murderer*, would go unrebuked, uncondemned.

All articles on this subject that I have read have been from men. They denounce women as alone guilty, and never include man in any plans proposed for the remedy of the evil.

It is clear to my mind that this evil wholly arises from the false position which woman occupies in civilized society. We know that in the brute creation, the female chooses her own time, and we are told that among Indians the woman does not permit the approach of the man during pregnancy or lactation; yet what Christian woman, wife of a Christian husband, is free to consult her own feelings, even in these most delicate situations?

Guilty? Yes, no matter what the motive, love of ease, or a desire to save from suffering the unborn innocent, the woman is awfully guilty who commits the deed. It will burden her conscience in life, it will burden her soul in death; but oh! thrice guilty is he who, for selfish gratification, heedless of her prayers, indifferent to her fate, drove her to the desperation which impelled her to the crime. It is very fine to say:

My Author and Disposer, what
  thou willst
Unquestioned I obey—Thus God
  ordains.
God is thy law, thou mine.

But God has never given woman's individuality into the hands of man. If He has, why hold her responsible for this crime? If man takes her individuality he must also take her responsibility. Let him suffer.

No, I say, yield to woman her God-given right of individuality. Make her feel that to God alone is she responsible for her deeds; teach her that submission to any man without love and desire is prostitution; and thunder in her ear, "Who so denieth the body, denieth the temple of the Holy Ghost!" let maternity come to her from a desire to cherish love and train for high purposes an immortal soul, then you will have begun to eradicate this most monstrous crime.

Men Must Open Their Eyes

Teach man to respect womanhood whether in the person of his own wife or the wife of another; teach him that as often as he outrages his wife he outrages Nature and disobeys the Divine Law, then you will have accomplished still more.

Oh, there is a dreadful volume of heart-histories that lies hidden in almost every family in the land! It tells of trust betrayed, of purity violated under sanction of law, of every holy feeling outraged and purest love turned to fear and loathing.

If the moral feeling in the heart of woman was not stronger than death itself, the crimes we now chronicle against them would be virtues compared with the depths of wickedness and sin into which they would be driven. But God is stronger than man and he holds us true to our highest natures, martyrs though we be. If, on the other hand, women were not so weak and disgracefully submissive, they would rise to the dignity of womanhood and, throwing off the degrading touch, would say, "I am free. And to God alone will I unquestioningly yield myself."

I believe all that is needed is for the eyes of men to be opened to the true states of affairs. They have received without a thought the faith of their fathers. The misery and degradation have not been personally felt by them. But let every wife dare to be honest, let her open her heart freely to her husband, and I know there are few whose better natures would not be touched, few who would not be awakened to a nobler life, to a more exalted view of marriage.

Then would marriage assume its high and holy place. Then would our children be truly olive plants, types of peace, lovingly desired, tenderly cared for, body and soul. Then the wife, looking with love and respect upon the husband, who has never caused her to fear his manhood, could say: "I am thine, and these are they whom God at our desire has given us."

The Conversion of Norma "Jane Roe" McCorvey

Norma McCorvey, with Gary Thomas

Norma McCorvey was "Jane Roe" in the landmark Roe v. Wade *Supreme Court decision that legalized abortion. Pregnant and desperate, she signed on to be the plaintiff in the famous case, and she continued working as an abortion-rights activist after the case was decided. In the following selection McCorvey describes in her own words her consternation when the antiabortion group Operation Rescue moved in next door to her office. However, after many conversations with the leader of Operation Rescue, McCorvey made a dramatic reversal; she was baptized a Christian and became staunchly antiabortion. McCorvey now runs Roe No More Ministry, assisting other pro-life organizations. Gary Thomas is coauthor along with McCorvey of* Won by Love, *the story of McCorvey's conversion.*

I could out-cuss the most crass of men and women; I could out-drink many of the Dallas taverns' regulars; and I was known for my hot temper. When pro-lifers called me a murderer, I called them worse. When people held up signs of aborted fetuses, I spit in their face.

I had a reputation to protect, after all. As the plaintiff in the infamous Supreme Court case *Roe v. Wade*, my life was inextricably tied up with abortion. Though I had never had one, abortion was the sun around which my life orbited. I once told a reporter, "This issue is the only thing I live for. I live, eat, breathe, think everything about abortion."

Then the fiery pro-life group Operation Rescue moved in next door.

Norma McCorvey, with Gary Thomas, " *Roe v. McCorvey*," www.leaderu.com. Copyright © by Roe No More Ministry. Reproduced by permission.

An Unlikely Friendship

I called Flip Benham, the brash and bold leader of Operation Rescue, Flip "Venom." Flip called me "responsible for the deaths of 35 million children." We were supposed to be sworn enemies, but due to the persistence of a local real estate agent, we became next door neighbors whose offices shared a common wall.

I will never forget the call I received on March 31, 1995, informing me about the move. I immediately lit up a second cigarette, even though I already had one burning. They don't make nicotine strong enough for situations such as these. Once my nerves were steadied, I called my contacts at CNN, and the media circus began almost immediately.

A Choice for Women was located in North Dallas. The aging one-story office building is U-shaped with a huge parking lot in the center. The abortion clinic was at the bottom of the U, set back about a hundred yards from any public walkway. That wasn't by accident. The abortion clinic owner wanted as much private property as possible between his front door and the sidewalk—where Operation Rescue and other pro-life demonstrators could legally gather.

The Dallas police settled down to an almost hourly routine. The bleep-bleep of a police siren and the flashing blue lights could be heard and seen several times a day for the next few months as O.R. and the abortion clinic clashed out in the parking lot.

Occasionally, the clashes would collapse into conversation. During one friendly banter, I goaded Flip, "What you need is to go to a good Beach Boys concert." Flip answered, "Miss Norma, I haven't been to a Beach Boys concert since 1976." The seemingly innocuous response shook me to the core. All at once, Flip became human to me.

Before, I had thought of Flip as a man who did nothing but yell at abortion clinics and read his Bible. In fact, I even pictured him sleeping with his hands across his chest, Dracula-like, with a big Bible tucked under his arms. The thought that he was a real person—a guy who had once even gone to a Beach Boys concert—never occurred to me. Now that it had, I saw him in a new light.

I continued the teasing. "Come on, Flip, I didn't know you were ever a sinner." "Miss Norma," Flip said, "I'm a great big sinner, saved by a great big God." Of all the things I expected Flip to say, this wasn't one of them. I didn't like to think of Flip as human.

But this "unreal" Flip was telling me that he was a sinner, that he had even gone to a Beach Boys concert! I couldn't connect that with the "fanatics" I had made the rescuers out to be; and it took a while for me to look past the confrontational tactics for which Flip was known. As we chatted outside on the bench between our offices, however, Flip began sharing some stories of his past and out of this vulnerability an unlikely friendship was born.

Other O.R. volunteers also began reaching out to me, dropping Scriptures and snippets of the Gospel at my feet whenever I seemed willing to receive them. In return, I explained my crystals and book of Runes. It wasn't exactly Elijah and the prophets of Baal, but in both of our minds it was clearly a case of "may the true God win."

A Child's Influence

As my mind was challenged to consider the truth of the Gospel, God began working on my heart through a 7-year-old girl named Emily, the daughter of O.R. volunteer Ronda Mackey.

Quite understandably, I had difficulty relating to children. I had given birth to three, all of whom had been placed for adoption (one of them against my will). And because I worked in an abortion clinic, I was fearful of bonding with anyone so young. It was part of my denial. When you know what is happening to the children behind closed doors, it's difficult to become attached to them outside.

Emily's blatant affection, frequent hugs, and direct pursuit disarmed me. The little girl's interest was all the more surprising considering Emily made it very clear that her acceptance of me wasn't an acceptance of my lifestyle. Early on in our relationship, I explained to Emily, "I like kids and wouldn't let anyone hurt little kids," to which Emily responded, "Then why do you let them kill the babies at the clinic?"

On another occasion, I invited Emily into my office. As I made appointments, Emily kept herself occupied. During one phone call, I lost my temper and said to a caller, "I'd just as soon see you in hell as see you in here," and Emily responded, "You don't have to go to hell, Miss Norma. You can pray right now and Jesus will forgive you."

This childlike faith cut open my heart, making me receptive to the truth being shared by the adult volunteers at Rescue. I wasn't won over by compelling apologetics. I had a ninth grade education and a very soft heart. While the O.R. adults targeted my mind, Emily went straight for the heart. And over time, Emily began to personify the issue of abortion—especially when Ronda broke down and told me that Emily had almost been aborted.

The Face of Abortion

Ronda was engaged when Emily was conceived, and nobody was very happy about it. Ronda's future in-laws, her mother, and her fiancee all pressured her to get an abortion during the first trimester. Ronda admits that she gave abortion serious consideration, at one point even giving her verbal assent to pursue it; but her memories of a high school friend's emotional devastation following an abortion strengthened Ronda's resolve to let Emily live.

Shortly after Ronda told me the long form of this story, I was walking outside a furniture store, shopping with Ronda and the girls. I have a decidedly mystical bent to my nature, and I was stunned when I saw Ronda's bumper sticker, "Abortion Stops a Beating Heart," which has a vividly red heart on the side.

All the sudden, I saw *Emily's* heart in that sticker, and it just about destroyed me when I realized that "my law" (as I once fondly referred to *Roe v. Wade*) had almost snuffed out young Emily's life. I asked to be taken home immediately, but later that afternoon, I spent over an hour on the phone with Ronda and a deep friendship was solidified.

I was forever changed by this experience. Abortion was no longer an "abstract right." It had a face now, in a little girl named Emily.

Ready for a Change

Emotionally, I was ready for a change. My alienation with the abortion movement was practically legendary, even before I became a Christian. Most of the abortion advocacy movement was afraid of my blue collar, tough-talking and unrefined ways. I was raised as a poor Louisiana girl who spent a good part of my childhood in reform schools. I ran away from home when I was ten, and spent several decades supporting myself with odd jobs—a carnival barker, a waitress, a bartender, cleaning apartments, construction work, and the like.

I spoke my mind, and the abortion movement's leadership kept as wide a hedge around me as possible. I wasn't asked to address the huge 1989 march in Washington, nor was I even invited to the 1993 twentieth anniversary celebration of *Roe v Wade*, held at the White House.

Such a blatant snub had understandable roots. I had publicly embarrassed [president emeritus of NARAL Pro-Choice America] Kate Michelman during Senate hearings over the Supreme Court nomination of David Souter. I had experienced a raucous falling out with my attorney, Sarah Weddington, whom I believed had "dumped" me. And I frequently caught abortion clinic directors off-guard by openly questioning the morality of some (particularly late-term) abortions. The fall-out with Weddington hurt me the most. I was chosen [to sign the affidavit] because Sarah Weddington needed someone who would sign the paper and fade into the background, never coming out and always keeping silent.

As my friendship with Flip drew national attention, I started receiving even more ridicule from my abortion advocate "friends." I soon found myself in the uncomfortable situation of being increasingly alienated from those on my side of the issue, and befriended by my alleged "enemies." Before long, I started coming to work simply so I could talk to the rescuers. I was scheduled to work just two days a week, but, I couldn't wait that long to get one of Emily's hugs.

Confusing Thoughts

It might bother some that the story of my actual conversion does not mimic the intellectual engagement of Augustine's "take and read," Pascal's wager, or C.S Lewis' famous motorcycle ride. I had a much different disposition, and I was challenged by a more "mystical" approach.

"Weird" things started to happen. My co-workers began hearing the sound of "little babies running down the hall." I went out one morning to cut some wild sunflowers for the recovery room, and I was certain I heard a little baby's laugh. I tore into the bush, scratching my arms, looking for the child, but found nothing but leaves. I looked up into the sky and said, "Okay, God, I don't know what you're doing up there, but I wish you would stop this. It isn't funny."

My spontaneous prayer shocked me as much as had the bush's laughter. I never talked to God. Had no reason to. He was sort of the enemy, after all. So what was I doing talking to Him now?

That day, a dull sadness came over me. I wasn't panicked anymore, I was just very, very sad, as if I were mourning the death of something precious. It came suddenly, strong enough to physically hurt my heart. I felt like a really close friend had died, or that many close friends had died—but nobody came to mind. Still, I couldn't shake the sadness.

I went home and spent the rest of the day sitting on my front porch. When my friend, Connie Gonzales, came home, she took one look at me and asked, "Are you okay?" I looked half-dead as I responded in a dead-panned voice, "I'm fine. I think I'm losing my mind, but I'm okay."

The confrontation between rescue volunteers and the abortion clinic workers became particularly acute on Thursdays through Saturdays, when abortions were actually performed. I was torn apart by the fact that for four days out of the week, myself and Ronda (not to mention the other volunteers at Rescue) were the best of friends, but on the other three we were bitter enemies.

During one abortion day confrontation, I charged up to Anne Hollacher, an O.R. volunteer who was holding a picket sign, and yelled, "You can't park on the same place you're picketing. Move the car!" "No, I'm not moving my car," Anne responded. "This is our parking lot too."

I called Anne every name I could think of, which was usually enough to make the toughest protesters wilt, but Anne maintained her composure. When I saw that Anne wouldn't budge, I spit in her face. Anne smiled. I was furious. "How dare you look at me like that?" I screamed. "How dare you smile at me?" Anne politely wiped the spit off her face with her sleeve. "Jesus loves you and so do I" she said. "And I forgive you."

It would have taken several clinic workers to pull me away from Anne except that I suddenly experienced severe chest pains and had to remove myself from the scene to catch my breath. Five minutes later, Ronda and the girls showed up, the girls eager to give me a hug, and I was overwhelmed by such a generous display of love after I had nursed so bitter a hatred. The confusion inside me became intense. I couldn't stand the thought of losing Ronda's friendship, and I wasn't about to let Emily be taken out of my life. But how long could we maintain a friendship when abortion stood between us?

Undoing Evil

"Miss Norma," Emily cooed one afternoon, "it would be sooo cool if you would come to church with us." I didn't want to disappoint Emily directly, so I answered, "Well, Emily, we'll have to be cool another time. I can't go to church with you this weekend." If I didn't want to offend Emily by an abrupt denial, I needn't have worried. Emily wasn't about to give up. Every morning, Ronda heard Emily pray, "Dear God, please don't let any babies be killed and make it so that abortion will end. And help miss Norma to come to Jesus."

Ronda didn't want Emily to be disillusioned about God not answering her prayers, so she explained, "God always answers our prayers, Emily, but Miss Norma has a choice to make here. She probably won't choose to follow Jesus. That's Miss Norma's fault, not God's. I don't want you to think God isn't listening to your prayers simply because Miss Norma doesn't become a Christian." Emily smiled. "She's going [to] come to know Jesus, mama." And with the faith of a child, Emily kept asking if I would come with her to church.

Finally, I said yes. I didn't agree to go to church out of a sudden need for God in my life. I just grew tired of telling Emily "no," so I said "yes." Ronda was skeptical. "*Norma? In church?*" But when they went to pick me up, I was dressed and ready to go.

Whatever my reasons for going, one sermon was all I needed. Pastor Morris Sheats of Hillcrest Church ended his sermon with a compelling evangelistic call from John 3:16 asking, "Is anyone here tired of living a sinner's life?" Immediately I felt overwhelmed with my need to respond.

How could I say no? I had been tired of it for years, but it was the only life I knew! I cautiously raised my hand, then opened my eyes and looked up to see if that really was my hand raised up high. It was. I couldn't believe it. I walked forward, leaning heavily on Ronda for support.

When I reached Pastor Sheats, I saw Jesus in his eyes. It made me feel so incredibly sorry for all my sins, especially for my role in legalizing abortion. I just kept repeating over and over, "I just want to undo all the evil I've done in this world. I'm so sorry, God. I'm so, so sorry. As far as abortion is concerned, I just want to undo it. I want it all to just go away." Finally, I stopped crying and broke into the biggest smile of my life. I no longer felt the pressure of my sin pushing down on my shoulders. The release was so quick that I felt like I could almost float outside.

Though abortion was tied up in my repentance, the political ramifications of my conversion wouldn't follow for several weeks.

A Crushing Realization

When my conversion became public knowledge, I spoke openly to reporters about still supporting legalized abortion in the first trimester. The media was quick to use this to downplay the seriousness of my conversion, saying I typified the "general ambivalence" of our culture over abortion. But a few weeks after my conversion, I was sitting in O.R.'s offices when I noticed a fetal development poster. The progression was so obvious, the eyes were so sweet. It hurt my heart, just looking at them.

I ran outside and finally, it dawned on me. "*Norma*," I said to myself, "*They're right.*" I had worked with pregnant women for years. I had been through three pregnancies and deliveries myself. I should have known. Yet something in that poster made me lose my breath. I kept seeing the picture of that tiny, 10-week-old embryo, and I said to myself, that's a baby! It's as if blinders just fell off my eyes and I suddenly understood the truth—that's a baby!

I felt "crushed" under the truth of this realization. I had to face up to the awful reality. Abortion wasn't about "products of conception." It wasn't about "missed periods." It was about children being killed in their mother's wombs. All those years I was wrong. Signing that affidavit, I was wrong. Working in an abortion clinic, I was wrong. No more of this first trimester, second trimester, third trimester stuff. Abortion—at any point—was wrong. It was so clear. Painfully clear.

One Hundred Percent Pro-Life

Two years after my conversion, I have since left Operation Rescue. After a grueling eleven-day encounter in San Diego in 1996, I began having serious reservations about whether I was cut out for the intense confrontations which often face Rescue volunteers. Because of my loyalty and affection for the people involved in Rescue, however, it took me until the early summer of 1997 to make the break complete.

Though every "re-alignment" creates tension, I am still appreciative and respectful toward Flip. Ronda Mackey has joined me in leaving O.R. and the two of us have set up a ministry to handle my increasing invitations to speak and appear at various pro-life events. Instead of being under the O.R. umbrella, I now report regularly to the pastors at Hillcrest Church.

My conversion is one for the ages. The timing was precise—O.R. was next door to my clinic for less than a year (Flip has said, "We moved in just long enough to pick up Miss Norma")—but it wasn't until I had a regenerated heart that the truth of what abortion does could find a place in my intellect. Once that truth took hold, there was no turning back.

"I'm one hundred percent sold out to Jesus and one hundred percent pro-life," I like to say. "No exceptions. No compromise."

Eugenic Abortion Is Unacceptable

George Neumayr

Eugenics, the improvement of the human race by selective breeding, is reducing the number of disabled infants, George Neumayr argues in the following viewpoint. He decries the practice of aborting embryos that are identified through prenatal screening as having disabilities such as Down syndrome, cystic fibrosis, and spina bifida. Neumayr suggests that it is a short step from eugenic abortion to custom-designing embryos to suit parents' desires. Neumayr is executive editor of the American Spectator.

Each year in America fewer and fewer disabled infants are born. The reason is eugenic abortion. Doctors and their patients use prenatal technology to screen unborn children for disabilities, then they use that information to abort a high percentage of them. Without much scrutiny or debate, a eugenics designed to weed out the disabled has become commonplace.

Not wishing to publicize a practice most doctors prefer to keep secret, the medical community releases only sketchy information on the frequency of eugenic abortion against the disabled. But to the extent that the numbers are known, they indicate that the vast majority of unborn children prenatally diagnosed as disabled are killed.

Medical researchers estimate that 80 percent or more of babies now prenatally diagnosed with Down syndrome are aborted. (They estimate that since 1989 70 percent of Down-syndrome fetuses have been aborted.) A high percentage of fetuses with cystic fibrosis are aborted, as evident in Kaiser Permanente's admission to the *New York Times* that 95 percent

George Neumayr, "The New Eugenics," *The American Spectator,* June 2005, pp. 22–25.
Copyright © 2005 by *The American Spectator.* Reproduced by permission.

of its patients in Northern California choose abortion after they find out through prenatal screening that their fetus will have the disease.

The frequent use of eugenic abortion can also be measured in dwindling populations with certain disabilities. Since the 1960s, the number of Americans with spina bifida has markedly declined. This dropping trend line corresponds to the rise of prenatal screening. Owing to prenatal technology and eugenic abortion, some rare conditions, such as the genetic disorder Tay-Sachs, are even vanishing in America, according to doctors.

"There really isn't any entity that is charged with monitoring what has been happening," says Andrew Imparato, head of the American Association of People with Disabilities (AAPD), "A lot of people prefer that that data not be collected. But we're seeing just the tip of the iceberg. This is a new eugenics, and I don't know where it is going to end."

Arguments Spark Public Outcry

"I think of it as commercial eugenics," says Andrew Kimbrell, executive director of the International Center for Technology Assessment. "Whenever anybody thinks of eugenics, they think of Adolf Hitler. This is a commercial eugenics. But the result is the same, an intolerance for those who don't fit the norm. It is less open and more subtle. Try to get any numbers on reproductive issues. Try to get actual numbers on sex-selection abortions. They are always difficult to get. If you are involved in that commerce, do you really want people to go: So you aborted how many disabled children? That's the last piece of information people want out there."

Indeed, intellectual arguments in favor of eugenic abortion often generate great public outcry. Princeton professor Peter Singer drew fire for saying, "It does not seem quite wise to increase any further draining of limited resources by increasing the number of children with impairments." Bob Edwards, the embryologist who created the first test-tube baby through in vitro fertilization, has also drawn protests for predicting that "soon it will be a sin of parents to have a child that carries the heavy burden of genetic disease. We are entering a world where we have to consider the quality of our children."

Pregnancies Gone Awry

But these comments, far from being unthinkable, reflect unspoken mainstream attitudes and practice. Only through political gaffes (and occasional news stories) is eugenic abortion ever mentioned, such as the time in 2003 when a blundering Hillary Clinton objected to a ban on partial-birth abortion because it didn't contain an exemption for late-term abortions aimed at the disabled. Women should not be "forced" to carry a "child with severe abnormalities," she said.

In an interview with *TAS* [*The American Spectator*], Senator Rick Santorum of Pennsylvania recalled his 2003 exchange with Hillary Clinton on the Senate floor in which she endorsed eugenic abortion. "It was pretty revealing. She was saying there had to be an exemption for disabled children being aborted as opposed to healthy children being aborted," he says. "When she realized what she was advocating for, she had to put in the general niceties. But I don't think you can read her comments and come to any other conclusion than that the children with disabilities should have less constitutional protection than children who are healthy."

He added that "the principal reason the Democrats defended the partial-birth abortion procedure was for pregnancies that have 'gone awry,' which is not about something bad happening to the life of the mother but about their finding out the child is not in the condition that they expected, that it was somehow less than wanted and what they had hoped for."

What Hillary Clinton blurted out is spoken more softly, though no less coldly, in the privacy of doctors' offices. Charles Strom, medical director of Quest Diagnostics, which specializes in prenatal screening, told the *New York Times* last year [2005] that "People are going to the doctor and saying, 'I don't want to have a handicapped child, what can you do for me?'" This attitude is shared by doctors who now view disabled infants and children as puzzling accidents that somehow slipped through the system. University of Chicago professor Leon Kass, in his book *Life, Liberty and the Defense of Dignity*, writes that "at my own university, a physician making rounds with medical students stood over the bed of an intelligent, otherwise normal ten-year-old boy with spina bifida. 'Were he to have been conceived today,' the physician casually informed his entourage, 'he would have been aborted.'"

Wrongful-Birth Lawsuits

The impulse behind prenatal screening in the 1970s was eugenic. After the *Roe v. Wade*[1] decision, which pumped energy into the eugenics movement, doctors scrambled to advance prenatal technology in response to consumer demand, mainly from parents who didn't want the burdens of raising children with Down syndrome. Now prenatal screening can identify hundreds of conditions. This has made it possible for doctors to abort children not only with chronic disabilities but common disabilities and minor ones. Among the aborted are children screened for deafness, blindness, dwarfism, cleft palates, and defective limbs.

In some cases the aborted children aren't disabled at all but are mere carriers of a disease or stand a chance of getting one later in life. Prenatal screening has made it possible to abort children on guesses and probabilities. A doctor speaking to the *New York Times* cited a defect for a eugenic abortion that was at once minor and speculative: a women suffering from a condition that gave her an extra finger asked doctors to abort two of her children on the grounds that they had a 50-50 chance of inheriting that condition.

1. *Roe v. Wade* legalized abortion.

The law and its indulgence of every conceivable form of litigation has also advanced the new eugenics against the disabled. Working under "liability alerts" from their companies, doctors feel pressure to provide extensive prenatal screening for every disability, lest parents or even disabled children hit them with "wrongful birth" and "wrongful life" suits. In a wrongful birth suit, parents can sue doctors for not informing them of their child's disability and seek compensation from them for all the costs, financial and otherwise, stemming from a life they would have aborted had they received that prenatal information. Wrongful life suits are brought by children (through their parents) against doctors for all the "damages" they've suffered from being born. (Most states recognize wrongful birth suits, but for many states, California and New Jersey among the exceptions, wrongful life suits are still too ridiculous to entertain.)

In 2003, Ob-Gyn Savita Khosla of Hackensack, New Jersey, agreed to pay $1.2 million to a couple and child after she failed to flag Fragile X syndrome, a form of mental retardation caused by a defective gene on the X chromosome. The mother felt entitled to sue Khosla because she indicated on a questionnaire that her sibling was mentally retarded and autistic, and hence Khosla should have known to perform prenatal screening for Fragile X so that she could abort the boy. Khosla settled, giving $475,000 to the parents and $750,000 to the child they wished that they had aborted.

Had the case gone to court, Khosla would have probably lost the suit. New Jersey has been notoriously welcoming to wrongful birth suits ever since the *Roe v. Wade* decision, after which New Jersey's Supreme Court announced that it would not "immunize from liability those in the medical field providing inadequate guidance to persons who would choose to exercise their constitutional right to abort fetuses which, if born, would suffer from genetic defects."

A Duty to Abort

According to the publication *Medical Malpractice Law & Strategy*, "court rulings across the country are showing that the increased use of genetic testing has substantially exposed physicians' liability for failure to counsel patients about hereditary disorders." The publication revealed that many wrongful birth cases "are settled confidentially." And it predicted that doctors who don't give their patients the information with which to consider the eugenic option against disabled children will face more lawsuits as prenatal screening becomes the norm. "The human genome has been completely mapped," it quotes Stephen Winnick, a lawyer who handled one of the first wrongful birth cases. "It's almost inevitable that there will be an increase in these cases."

The combination of doctors seeking to avoid lawsuits and parents seeking burden-free children means that once prenatal screening identifies a problem in a child the temptation to eugenic abortion becomes unstoppable. In an atmosphere of expected eugenics, even queasy, vaguely pro-life parents gravitate towards aborting a disabled child. These parents get pressure from doctors who, without even bothering to ask, automatically provide abortion options to them once the prenatal screening has diagnosed a disability (one parent, in a 1999 study, complained of a doctor showing her a video depicting the rigors of raising an afflicted child as a way of convincing her to choose abortion), and they feel pressure from society at large which having accepted eugenic abortion looks askance at parents with disabled children.

The right to abort a disabled child, in other words, is approaching the status of a duty to abort a disabled child. Parents who abort their disabled children won't be asked to justify their decision. Rather, it is the parents with disabled children who must justify themselves to a society that tacitly asks: Why did you bring into the world a child you knew was disabled or might become disabled?

Andrew Kimbrell points out that many parents are given the complicated information prenatal screening yields with little to no guidance from doctors. "We're leaving parents with complete confusion. Numerous parents are told by doctors, 'We think there is some fault on the 50th chromosome of your child.' A number of polls have shown that people don't understand those odds."

"There is enormous confusion out there and nobody is out there to help them," he says. "This is a huge tangle. And it leads people to abort out of confusion: 'I guess I better abort, because I don't know. It sounds really bad and I don't know what the percentages mean.'"

Promoting Desirable Embryos

The new eugenics isn't slowing down but speeding up. Not content to wait to see if a child is fit for life, doctors are exploring the more proactive eugenics of germline genetic engineering (which tries to create desirable traits in an embryo) and Preimplantation Genetic Diagnosis (PGD), which is used to select the most desirable embryos after extensive genetic testing has been done before they are implanted in mothers' wombs.

"The next stage is to actually start tinkering genetically with these embryos to create advantages such as height," says Kimbrell. PGD is a "gateway technology" that will advance the new eugenics to the point "where children are literally selected and eventually designed according to a parent's desires and fears," he says. (Meanwhile, doctors are simultaneously reporting that children born through in vitro fertilization are experiencing higher rates of birth defects than the average population, suggesting that for every problem scientists try to solve through dubious means they create multiple new ones.)

Many countries have banned PGD. But American fertility clinics are offering it. Two-thirds of fertility clinics using PGD in the world are in the U.S., says Kimbrell. "Reproductive technology is an unregulated Wild West scenario where people can do pretty much anything they want and how they want it," he says.

Charles Darwin's cousin, Francis Galton, coined the term eugenics in the 1880s. Sparking off his cousin's theory of evolution, he proposed improving the human race through eugenics, arguing that "what nature does blindly, slowly, and ruthlessly, man may do providently, quickly, and kindly." As eugenics passes through each of its stages—from sterilizing the enfeebled at the beginning of the 20th century to aborting the disabled at the end of it and the beginning of the 21st— man is indeed playing God but without any of his providence or care.

Andrew Imparato of AAPD wonders how progressives got to this point. The new eugenics aimed at the disabled unborn tell the disabled who are alive, "disability is a fate worse than death," he says. "What kind of message does this send to people living with spina bifida and other disabilities? It is not a progressive value to think that a disabled person is better off dead."

The Moral Case for Abortion

Henry Morgentaler

In the following selection Henry Morgentaler argues that many people today take abortion rights for granted, but in fact these rights are threatened by antiabortionists who depend on religious dogma rather than reason to inform their moral choices. He contends that legal access to abortion upholds women's right to control their own fertility. Abortion rights also benefit society, Morgentaler asserts. Abortion reduces the number of unwanted children, many of whom become criminals as a result of parental abuse or neglect. In sum, he says, abortion is moral because of the many benefits that accrue from it. Henry Morgentaler is the founding president of the Humanist Association of Canada and the author of Abortion and Contraception. *He has opened abortion clinics across Canada, often in the face of strong opposition.*

This is a very appropriate time for me to write on "The Moral Case for Abortion." Many people in the pro-choice community believe that the battle for reproductive freedom has been won, that abortion is now available, that women have gained control over their reproductive capacities and have been liberated from the repressive rulings of patriarchal governments. This is not completely true.

There are still many countries in the world where women are subjected to the dogmatic religious edicts of theocracies. There are still women willing to endanger their health, future fertility, and even their lives in order to terminate an unwanted pregnancy. The religious right and the anti-abortion movement is gaining ground on this continent and abroad. Even here, in the United States, where everyone hoped that

Henry Morgentaler, "The Moral Case for Abortion," *Free Inquiry,* Summer 1996. Copyright 1996 by the Council for Democratic and Secular Humanism, Inc. Reproduced by permission.

Roe v. Wade would forever ensure a woman's right to choice, the violent factions of the anti-abortion movement are waging war on doctors, staff, and abortion clinics; and political lobby groups and presidential candidates violently opposed to choice are within reach of the Oval Office. There are even members of the pro-choice community who are questioning the morality of reproductive freedom. These people believe that abortion must be available, but that it is inherently bad—a necessary evil. This attitude is dangerous and destructive and undermines the enormous gains due to the availability of good abortion services. In fact, the decision to have an abortion is clearly an extremely moral choice; it is a choice that liberates, empowers, and benefits women and society. In this article, I will examine all these issues from a humanist perspective, and reaffirm the morality of reproductive choice.

Dogma Versus Reason

The issue of the morality of abortion provides the best illustration of the profound difference between humanist ethics and traditional religious attitudes. The former are based on concern for individual and collective well-being and are able to incorporate all available modern data and knowledge; whereas the latter are bound by dogma and tradition to sexist, irrational prohibitions against abortion and women's rights and are completely and callously indifferent to the enormous, avoidable suffering such attitudes are inflicting on individuals and on the community.

Most of the debate raging about abortion around the world has centered around the question of morality. Is it ever moral or responsible for a woman to request and receive an abortion, or is abortion always immoral, sinful, and criminal?

When you listen to the rhetoric of the anti-abortion faction, or read imprecise terms about the unborn, you get the impression that every abortion kills a child; consequently it cannot be condoned under any circumstances, with the sole exception of when the life of the pregnant woman is endangered by the pregnancy, a condition that is now extremely rare. This position—that abortion is always wrong and that there is a human being in the womb from the moment of conception—is a religious idea mostly propagated by the doctrine of the Roman Catholic church and espoused by many fundamentalist Protestant groups, though not by the majority of Catholics and Protestants.

Let us briefly examine this idea. At the moment of conception the sperm and the ovum unite, creating one cell. To proclaim that this one cell is already a full human being and should be treated as such is so patently absurd that it is almost difficult to refute. It is as if someone claimed that one brick is already a house and should be treated with the same respect a full house deserves. Even if you have a hundred bricks, or two hundred bricks, it is not yet a house. For it to be a house it needs walls, plumbing, electricity, and a functional organization. The same is true for a developing embryo. In order for it to be a human being it needs an internal organization, organs, and especially a human brain to be considered fully human. This entity is the result of sexual intercourse, where procreation is often not the goal, and whether it is called a zygote, blastocyst, embryo, or fetus, it does not have all the attributes of a human being and thus cannot properly be considered one.

If abortion is always viewed as "intentional murder," why isn't miscarriage viewed in similar terms? After all, almost half of all embryos are spontaneously shed in what is called "miscarriage" or "spontaneous abortion." If spontaneous abortions are an "act of God," to use the common religious expression, is it not strange that God has so little concern for fetal life that He allows so much of it to go to waste without intervening? Is it not possible to then conclude that God does not mind or object to spontaneous abortions? Why is it that the Catholic church has no ritual to mark the abortion of so much fetal life when it occurs spontaneously, yet becomes so vociferous and condemnatory when it is a conscious decision by a woman or couple?

Potential Human Beings

I believe that an early embryo may be called a potential human being. But remember that every woman has the potential to create twenty-five human beings in her lifetime. The idea that any woman who becomes pregnant as a result of non-procreative sexual intercourse must continue with her pregnancy does not take into consideration the fact that there is a tremendous discrepancy between the enormous potential of human fertility and the real-life ability of women and couples to provide all that is necessary to bring up children properly. The morality of any act cannot be divorced from the foreseeable consequences of that act. Should a girl of twelve or a woman of forty-five, or any woman for that matter, be forced to continue a pregnancy or be saddled with bringing up a child for eighteen years without any regard for the consequences, without any regard for the expressed will or desire of that woman, or of the couple?

Haven't we learned anything by observing events in countries where abortion is illegal, where women are forced to abort fetuses themselves or by the hands of quacks, where many die and more are injured for life or lose their fertility? What about the children often abandoned to institutions where they have no father or mother, where they suffer so much emotional deprivation and trauma that many become psychotic, neurotic, or so full of hate and violence that they become juvenile delinquents and criminals who kill, rape, and maim? When a person is treated badly in his or her childhood, that inner violence manifests itself when he or she is grown up.

The pro-choice philosophy maintains that the availability of good medical abortions protects the health and fertility of women and allows children to be born into homes where they can receive love, care, affection, and respect for their unique individuality, so that these children grow up to be joyful, loving, caring, responsible members of the community, able to enter into meaningful relationships with others.

Reproductive Freedom Protects Women

Thus, reproductive freedom—access to legal abortions, to contraception, and, by extension, to sexual education—protects women and couples and is probably the most important aspect of preventive medicine and psychiatry, as well as the most promising preventative of crime and mental illness in our society.

Wherever abortion legislation has been liberalized, particularly in countries where abortion is available upon request, the effects on public health and on the well-being of the community have been very positive. The drastic reduction of illegal, incompetent abortions with their disastrous consequences has almost eliminated one of the major hazards to the lives and health of fertile women. There has been a steady decline in the complications and mortality associated with medical abortions, a decline in mortality due to childbirth, a drop in newborn and infant mortality, an overall decline in premature births, and a drop in the number of births of unwanted children. It is of utmost interest to examine the consequences and effects of the liberalization of the abortion laws.

Where abortion has become legalized and available and where there is sufficient medical manpower to provide quality medical services in this area, the consequences have all been beneficial not only to individuals but also to society in general. In countries where there is a high level of education and where abortions by qualified medical doctors are available without delay, self-induced or illegal abortions by incompetent people who do not have medical knowledge eventually disappear, with tremendous benefit to the health of women. Also, the mortality connected to medical legal abortions decreases to an amazing degree. In Czechoslovakia in 1978, for instance, the mortality rate was two per 100,000 cases; in the United States it was one death per 200,000 abortions, which is extremely low and compares favorably with the mortality rate for most surgical procedures.

Another medical benefit is that the mortality of women in childbirth also decreases in countries where abortion is legal and the medical manpower exists to provide quality services. This is because the high-risk patients like adolescents, older women, and women with diseases often choose not to continue a high risk pregnancy; consequently, the women who go through childbirth are healthier and better able to withstand the stresses of childbirth; thus, the infant mortality and neonatal mortality has decreased consistently in all countries where abortion has become available.

But probably the biggest benefit of legalized abortion and the one with the greatest impact is that the number of unwanted children is decreasing. Children who are abused, brutalized, or neglected are more likely to become neurotic, psychotic, or criminal elements of society. They become individuals who do not care about themselves or others, who are prone to violence, who are filled with hatred for society and for other people; if the number of such individuals decreases, the welfare of society increases proportionately.

A Decrease in Crime

One of the most surprising and beneficial changes going on in both the United States and Canada has been the tremendous decrease in crime, especially violent crime such as murder, rape, and aggravated assault. This trend over the last four years has been proven by impressive statistics collected by the Federal Bureau of Investigators and the police forces of the United States and Canada. The decrease in violent crime is about 8% every year over the last four years. That is quite an impressive trend. Statistics from the province of Quebec, just released April 4, 1996, show a decrease in criminal offenses of 15% every year over the last three years and a decrease of 8% for violent crime. There has been a 30% decrease in crime in New York State, e.g. and many similar statistics in other areas are surprising and extraordinary in view of the prevailing economic uncertainties and disruptions of modern life. What is the explanation?

Some demographers explain this by the fact that there are fewer young men around, and it is mostly young men who commit crimes. No doubt this is true, but what is even more important is that among these young men likely to commit offenses there are fewer who carry an inner rage and vengeance in their hearts from having been abused or cruelly treated as children.

Why is that? Because many women who a generation ago were obliged to carry any pregnancy to term now have had the opportunity to choose medical abortion when they were not ready to assume the burden and obligations of motherhood.

Crimes of violence are very often perpetrated by persons who unconsciously want revenge for the wrongs they suffered as children. This need to satisfy an inner urge for vengeance results in violence against children, women, members of minority groups, or anyone who becomes a target of hate by the perpetrator. Children who have been deprived of love and good care, who have been neglected or abused, suffer tremendous emotional harm that may cause mental illness, difficulty in living, and an inner rage that eventually erupts in violence when they become adolescents and adults.

Most of the serial killers were neglected and abused children, deprived of love. Paul Bernardo and Clifford Olson would fit in that category. Both Hitler and Stalin were cruelly beaten by their fathers and carried so much hate in their hearts that when they attained power they caused millions of people to die without remorse. It is accepted wisdom that prevention is better than a cure. To prevent the birth of unwanted children by family planning, birth control, and abortion is preventive medicine, preventive psychiatry, and prevention of violent crime.

I predicted a decline in crime and mental illness twenty-five years ago when I started my campaign to make abortion in Canada legal and safe. It took a long time for this prediction to come true. I expect that conditions will get better as more and more children are born into families that want and deserve them with joy and anticipation.

Decrease in Mental Illness

It is safe to assume that there has been a similar decrease in mental and emotional illness due to the fact that fewer unwanted children are being born. Consequently fewer children suffer the emotional deprivation or abuse that is often associated with being unwanted and undesired. It would be interesting to see appropriate studies to that effect, and I postulate that they would show a dramatic decrease in the overall incidence of mental illness.

Medical abortions on request and good quality care in this area are a tremendous advance not only toward individual health and the dignity of women, but also toward a more loving, caring, and more responsible society, a society where cooperation rather than violence will prevail. Indeed, it may be our only hope to survive as a human species and to preserve intelligent life on this planet in view of the enormous destructive power that mankind has accumulated.

The right to legal abortion is a relatively new achievement, only about twenty-five years old in most countries. It is part of the growing movement of women toward emancipation, toward achieving equal status with men, toward being recognized as full, responsible, equal members of society. We are living in an era where women, especially in the Western world, are being recognized as equal, where the enormous human potential of womankind is finally being acknowledged and accepted as a valuable reservoir of talent. However, women cannot achieve their full potential unless they have freedom to control their bodies, to control their reproductive capacity. Unless they have access to safe abortions to correct the vagaries of biological accidents, they cannot pursue careers, they cannot be equal to men, they cannot avail themselves of the various opportunities theoretically open to all members of our species. The emancipation of women is not possible without reproductive freedom.

The full acceptance of women might have the enormous consequence of humanizing our species, possibly eliminating war and conflict, and adding a new dimension to the adventure of mankind. Civilization has had many periods of advance and regression, but overall it has seen an almost steady progression toward the recognition of minorities as being human and their acceptance into the overall community. It has happened with people of different nationalities and races. It has happened with prisoners of war, who could be treated mercilessly. It has happened quite recently, actually, with children, who were in many societies considered the property of parents and could be treated with brutality and senseless neglect. It is only a few generations ago that we recognized how important it is for society to treat children with respect, care, love, and affection, so that they become caring, loving, affectionate, responsible adults.

Finally, many countries now recognize the rights of women to belong fully to the human species, and have given them freedom from reproductive bondage and allowed them to control their fertility and their own bodies. This is a revolutionary advance of great potential significance to the human species. We are in the middle of this revolution, and it is not surprising that many elements of our society are recalcitrant and are obstructing this progress. They act out of blind obedience to dogma, tradition, and past conditions and are hankering for the times when women were oppressed and considered only useful for procreation, housework, and the care of children.

Solving the World's Real Problems

The real problems in the world—starvation, misery, poverty, and the potential for global violence and destruction—call for concerted action on the part of governments, institutions, and society at large to effectively control overpopulation. It is imperative to control human fertility and to only have children who can be well taken care of, receiving not only food, shelter, and education, but also the emotional sustenance that comes from a loving home and parents who can provide love, affection, and care.

In order to achieve this, women across the world have to be granted the rights and dignity they deserve as full members of the human community. This would naturally include the right to safe medical abortions on request in an atmosphere of acceptance of specifically female needs and in the spirit of the full equality of women and men in a more human and humane society.

Somebody has said that it is impossible to stop the success of an idea whose time has come. But good ideas come and go. Occasionally they are submerged for long periods of time due to ignorance, tradition, resistance to change, and the vested interests of those frightened by change. Occasionally, new and good ideas will gain slow and grudging acceptance. More often, they will be accepted only after a period of struggle and sacrifice by those who are convinced of the justice of their cause. The struggle for reproductive freedom, including the right to safe, medical abortion, could be classified as one of those great ideas whose time has come.

Enormous progress has been made in many countries, including the United States and Canada. But in many other countries, legal abortion is still not available. With the beneficial effects of women's access to abortion and reproductive freedom so obvious to so many people, why is there still so much violent opposition to it? I believe it is due to the fact that people who are bound to traditional religious attitudes resent the newly acquired freedom of women and want to turn the clock back.

Taboos and practices regarding human reproduction and sexuality were written into religious teachings hundreds of years ago, which were then written into the laws of the country. Laws on abortion were introduced long before science enlightened us with the facts concerning embryological development. For instance, in the Catholic church it was thought that, at the moment of conception, a fully formed person, termed a homunculus, lived in the mother's womb, and had only to develop to a certain size to be expelled from it. That belief was held in the distant past, but the effect of the imagery still remains, resulting in the Catholic belief that abortion is the murder of a live human being.

Historically, and even up to this day, men hold the authority in all the major religions of the world. In most countries men are also heads of state and lawmakers. In science and medicine, men traditionally hold the reins of authority and power, only recently allowing women entry into these fields. Is it any wonder then, that laws and attitudes regarding abortion took so long to change? But now these attitudes are changing, and women around the world are gradually acquiring more power and more control of their reproductive capacities. Unfortunately, organized religions, propelled by traditional dogma and fundamentalist rhetoric, are fueling the fires of the anti-choice movement with lying, inflammatory propaganda and violent rhetoric leading to riots and murder. The anti-choice supporters realize they have lost the battle, that public opinion has not been swayed by their diatribes and dogmatic opposition. Consequently, they are angry and increasingly engaging in terrorist tactics. Their recourse to violence, both in the United States and Canada, resulting in the murder and wounding of doctors performing abortions and the increasing violence directed at abortion providers, is a sign of moral bankruptcy, but unfortunately it places the lives of all physicians and medical staff who provide abortions in danger.

Pro-Lifers Do Not Stand on the Moral High Ground

For those who believe that the so-called pro-life have occupied the high moral ground in the debate on abortion, I say, "Rubbish." They have never been on a high moral ground, they only pretend to occupy this elevated position by cloaking their oppressive beliefs under the lofty rhetoric of "the defense of innocent unborn life" or "the struggle against the death dealing abortion industry" and similar misleading and blatantly false propaganda. As well, the recourse by the anti-choice movement to violence and murder in order to impose their so-called morality on the whole of society certainly robs them of any credibility. In view of this, it is hard for me to understand the defeatist attitude of some people in the pro-choice community in the United States and their attempt to justify abortion as a necessary evil for which we should all apologize.

When a feminist with impressive credentials and many books to her credit such as Naomi Wolf talks of abortion as a "sin or frivolous," starts feeling guilty about it, and wants everyone who is engaged in providing abortions to repent for their sins, there is something definitely wrong. Were she alone I could believe it is a personal idiosyncrasy. However, there are others in the pro-choice community who attempt to justify themselves and their actions with an attitude that says, "Yes, we need abortions to help some women, but we deplore the fact that we have to do them, our hearts are not really in it, and it would be nice if we did not have to do it."

What is going on here? Have all these people forgotten that women used to die in our countries from self-induced or quack abortions, that unwanted children were given away to institutions where they suffered enormous trauma that took the joy of life away from them and made them into anxious, depressed, individuals with a grudge against society? Have all these people forgotten that an unwanted pregnancy was the biggest health hazard to young fertile women and could result in loss of fertility, long-term illness, injury, and death?

Let us keep in mind the positive accomplishments of reproductive freedom that I mentioned earlier. An abortion need not be a traumatic event; it often is a liberating experience for the woman, who is able to make an important decision in her life, who exercises her right to choose what is best for her. That is the meaning of freedom, of empowerment.

Empowerment and Liberation

A woman's choice to terminate a pregnancy is both empowering and liberating. It empowers her because her choice acknowledges that she understands her options, her current situation, and her future expectations, and she is able to make a fully informed decision about what would most benefit her and act on it. It liberates her because she can regain control of her reproductive system and chart her destiny without an unwanted child in tow. It liberates her to fully care for her existing family, her career, her emotional and mental well-being, and her goals.

It is our job as abortion providers to respect the choices of women and to provide abortion services with competence, compassion, and empathy. I wish to suggest that under such conditions women do not necessarily view their abortion as negative, but, on the contrary, and in spite of regrets at having to make such a choice, see it as a positive and enriching experience where their choices are respected and they are treated with the dignity they deserve in such a difficult situation.

Doctors and clinic workers have been in a stressful situation for many years, subject to threats, insults, and moral condemnation. Over the last four years the threats have escalated from verbal abuse to murder. Yet most of us have not given up. Most of us continue to provide excellent abortion services to women in spite of all the threats because we are committed to protection of women's health and to the liberation of women, to the empowerment of women and couples and to a better society with freedom for all. I wish to salute all those health professionals who, in spite of intimidation and threats of death, are continuing every day to treat women with competence, empathy, and compassion.

I wish to conclude on a personal note. Over the years many people have asked me: "Why did you decide to expose yourself to so much stress and danger in a controversial cause, and why do you persist in doing so?" The answer, after a great deal of reflecting upon it, is the following:

I am a survivor of the Nazi Holocaust, that orgy of cruelty and inhumanity of man to man. As such, I have personally experienced suffering, oppression, and justice inflicted by men beholden to an inhuman, dogmatic, irrational ideology. To relieve suffering, to diminish oppression and injustice, is very important to me. Reproductive freedom and good access to medical abortion means that women can give life to wanted babies at a time when they can provide love, care, and nurturing. Well-loved children grow into adults who do not build concentration camps, do not rape, and do not murder. They are likely to enjoy life, to love and care for each other and the larger society.

By fighting for reproductive freedom, I am contributing to a more caring and loving society based on the ideals of peace, justice, and freedom, and devoted to the full realization of human potential. Having known myself the depth of human depravity and cruelty, I wish to do whatever I can to replace hate with love, cruelty with kindness, and irrationality with reason.

This is why I am so passionately dedicated to the cause I defend and why I will continue to promote it as long as I have a valid contribution to offer.

CHAPTER 3

Abortion Activism

Chapter Preface

Activists on both sides of the abortion debate take various paths to advance their goals. Some activists engage in direct action. Others use the political process to work toward their goals. Finally, many activists work through religious institutions to get their arguments heard.

Although most activists work within legal boundaries, some individuals and groups have taken more direct and extreme actions. For example, Operation Rescue, an antiabortion organization active in the late 1980s and early 1990s, staged massive demonstrations at abortion clinics in an attempt to disrupt abortion services. Even more extreme were the antiabortion activists who bombed and burned clinics and murdered abortion doctors. Those in favor of abortion have limited themselves to nonviolent direct action, usually in the form of rallies at government buildings to protest the passage of bills restricting abortion rights.

Although bombings garner the most media attention, in fact most abortion activism is conducted through legal means. For example, activists routinely lobby Congress to gain votes for abortion-related bills they support. Candidates for public office are often subjected to what is commonly called a "litmus test," in which, through the course of their campaigns, they are grilled about their opinions about abortion. In the minds of abortion activists, this test is a measure of how effectively a candidate will advance their goals. Abortion proponents hope to elect officials who will protect a woman's right to choose abortion, while opponents seek to elect those who will pass legislation to further limit abortion.

Religious organizations have become active in the abortion debate as well. Many religious institutions favor abortion, while others, the Catholic Church in particular, take an active stance against abortion. These religious leaders exhort their parishioners to support only those political candidates who are steadfastly against abortion. Some Catholic politicians have been threatened with excommunication and denied communion because of their pro-choice views.

Like most people involved in social causes, abortion activists are varied, and thus, too, are their approaches. While some extreme activists engage in violent direct action, others work within the law to pass favorable legislation and elect friendly politicians. Religious activists often find that their messages are best disseminated through the churches they are affiliated with. As the social climate changes, activists discover that some means that worked in the past have become ineffective, and they begin trying other approaches. As the abortion controversy continues, it is likely that activists on both sides of the debate will utilize established methods for advancing their causes, and they may even attempt to use other means not yet tried.

The Founding of Planned Parenthood

Faye Wattleton

Faye Wattleton, a nurse, was the first African American to head the Planned Parenthood Federation of America and only the second woman to lead the organization after founder Margaret Sanger. In the following excerpt from Wattleton's autobiography, she traces the history of Planned Parenthood, which was incorporated in 1922 as the American Birth Control League. Planned Parenthood's policy today is to ensure that all individuals have the freedom to make reproductive decisions, and it has become an important abortion-rights advocacy group. Wattleton served as president of Planned Parenthood from 1978 to 1992. She is currently president of the Center for the Advancement of Women, an organization established to advance women's equal participation at every level of society.

On joining the board of Planned Parenthood, I had little sense of the organization, beyond the services it provided at its Columbus and Dayton clinics. I didn't know, and wouldn't know, until I became president of the Planned Parenthood Federation of America, that the organization had begun with one woman's fervent wish to empower women by freeing them from the limitations of uncontrolled childbearing.

Margaret Sanger was born in Corning, New York, in 1883. As a young woman, she served as a nurse in New York City, where she became appalled at the toll exacted on women's lives and bodies by self-induced abortion. But this was an era when many considered her ideas too crude, if not altogether heretical, to discuss in polite society. However, the late nine-

Faye Wattleton, *Life on the Line*. New York: Ballantine, 1996. Copyright © 1996 by Faye Wattleton. All rights reserved. Reproduced by permission.

teenth century was the time when the campaign for women's rights, led by such crusaders as Elizabeth Cady Stanton and Susan B. Anthony, had risen up against the Victorian cult of motherhood and the expected submission of women to the whims and desires of men. Perhaps realizing that the ideas they expressed were radical enough in themselves, these women did not speak to the legitimacy of a woman's own sexual needs. Neither did they challenge the idea that motherhood was the proper vocation of a woman. Instead, they advocated "voluntary motherhood," which included the unpopular views that men should curb their sexual urges and, more important, that a woman should be able to reject her husband's sexual advances. These early activists argued that if a woman could choose when to have children she would be a better mother, with better children. In this way, the voluntary motherhood movement laid the foundations for the public discussion of birth control.

Comstock Laws Oppressed Women

But the forces of oppression were not to move aside easily. Anthony Comstock, who was born in New England in 1844 and moved to New York City as a young man, launched a crusade to pass laws that would wipe out "vice and obscenity," which he perceived to be overtaking the city and the country at large. His vehicle to repress any advances made by the voluntary motherhood movement was the Society for the Suppression of Vice, which he founded in 1869. By 1873 Comstock had accumulated an impressive collection of pornographic material, which by his standards included any information about contraception and abortifacients, and he carted it to Washington to exhibit to members of the United States Congress. There the collection's detailed exposition received far more attention than it would have gotten otherwise. (One hundred years later, Senator Orrin Hatch and some of his colleagues orchestrated a similar demonstration, exhibiting films and sex education materials, and demanding that I answer for our violation of public morality.)

Comstock's presentation had its desired effect when the shocked senators and representatives passed a federal statute prohibiting the mailing of "every obscene, lewd, or lascivious, and every filthy book, pamphlet, picture, paper, letter, writing, print, or other publication ... designed, adapted, or intended for preventing conception or producing abortion, or for any indecent or immoral use." Many states extended the prohibitions to include the discussion, publication, or advertising of any information discussing contraception or abortion, and Connecticut outlawed contraception altogether. The federal laws and their state counterparts became known as the Comstock Laws, and they would continue to wield some influence until as late as 1983, when the last of the laws was struck down.

Poor Women Were Powerless

During the early years of the twentieth century, even as Comstock battled on, Margaret Sanger had taken her nursing practice to the tenements of New York City. It was clear to her that white wealthy women had long had the knowledge and the means to circumvent the Comstock Laws that made safe and effective contraception state and federal crimes; poor women did not. By the thousands, they suffered the debilitating and often fatal consequences of uncontrolled childbirth.

Sanger recognized that a woman's powerlessness could never be overcome without challenging the prevailing notion that her primary role in society, and even her duty, was to bear children. She and her colleagues, the unstoppable revolutionary Emma Goldman among them, set about making the birth control issue explicit in public and political forums. Like their predecessors, they didn't minimize the value of motherhood, but rather sought to provide women with the means to control their own fertility.

Sanger's passionate defense of women's reproductive rights must surely have been prompted by her mother's death after eighteen pregnancies. Later, she also recounted the case of a young woman who had begged her for information on contraception. Legally hamstrung, Sanger had been unable to answer her pleas, then learned that soon after her visit, the young woman had died from an illegal, self-induced abortion. Sanger claimed that the young woman's tragedy had played a pivotal role in shaping her vision of reform.

In 1914, when she was brought up on felony charges for her "obscene" views on women's sexuality and her revolutionary activities, she fled to Europe, leaving her husband and small children behind. In the more progressive circles abroad, Sanger honed her vision and her knowledge of contraceptive methods. She returned home to stand trial. However, after much visibility and public support had been generated, the charges were dismissed and Sanger returned to her work with zeal.

Sanger Opened the First Birth Control Clinic

In 1916 Sanger opened her first birth control clinic in the impoverished Brownsville section of Brooklyn. There, in the guise of "consultations," for which she charged ten cents, she offered contraceptives: diaphragms, condoms, suppositories, and the Mizpah Pessary, a device that blocked the opening to the womb, which was Sanger's recommended form of birth control. The demand for these services was, as Sanger had known it would be, overwhelming.

Ten days after the clinic's opening a police raid forced Sanger and her sister, Ethel Byrne, to close it down. Both women and a co-worker were arrested. Their subsequent trials and convictions for establishing the clinic and for giving out illegal information on contraception provoked a maelstrom of publicity. Cannily sensing that the publicity could be turned to their cause, Ethel staged a hunger strike in jail and was force-fed by prison authorities. Even Governor Charles S. Whitman entered the fray, offering to pardon all three miscreants if Margaret Sanger promised to stop all her birth control work. At first she refused the stipulation, but when she saw how weak her sister had become, she conceded to it. Her promise to the governor was one she would not be able to keep.

Despite the attention her work was receiving, Sanger later described the time between 1917 and 1921 as her "leaden years." She was constantly short of money for her cause, and her new magazine, *The Birth Control Review*, lost its mailing privileges. Rather than letting it die, she and her collaborators resorted to selling it on Times Square street corners. And the publicity surrounding her jailing had strengthened her opposition as much as it had rallied her supporters. Hotels that allowed her to speak in their conference rooms were boycotted. The mayor of Boston threatened to revoke the license of any establishment that allowed her to speak there. In response, she appeared at one gathering with a wide strip of white tape covering her mouth.

Even as Sanger's movement proceeded, women were working in concert to emancipate other aspects of their lives. In the upper and middle classes, they were determined to deconstruct the cloistering vestiges of Victorianism and to redefine women's social, political, and economic power. And women were achieving higher levels of formal education, and forging careers in professions that had formerly been reserved for men. But as far as Sanger was concerned, nothing was so fundamental to the establishment of women's equality as the freedom from sexual repression.

Birth Control Groups Began Forming

The first American birth control organization, the National Birth Control League [NBCL], had been created in 1915 by

Mary Ware Dennett in New York City. Although started by a liberal group, the organization did not want to be identified with Sanger and others with "radical" tactics. The NBCL dissolved only four years later, in 1919, when World War I turned public attention to other causes. Following the demise of the NBCL, Mary Ware Dennett organized the Voluntary Parenthood League, whose primary aim was to repeal the federal statutes on birth control.

Sanger would not join a group with so narrow a focus, nor one she had no hope of controlling. Her vision was of groups that would conduct federal and local legislative work and would also open clinics across the country and conduct research. Financed by Mrs. George Rublee, Mrs. Paul Cravath, Mrs. Dwight Morrow, and other prominent New York women, Sanger worked in 1920 and 1921 to organize the American Birth Control League. More support was consolidated from the well-to-do, many of whom were ardent libertarians, after police raided a meeting at Town Hall in which many of "their own" were taking part. Eventually the medical profession would also endorse the league.

In 1921, Sanger organized the first American Birth Control Conference which was held in New York City. Her movement quickly spread to other parts of the country as she traveled tirelessly to promote the creation of birth control clinics. By 1930, there were fifty-five centers in twenty-three cities in twelve states, from Bangor, Maine, to El Paso, Texas. In 1938, the courts removed a major barrier to the advancement of the birth control movement. Judge Augustus Hand of the Second Circuit Court of Appeals in New York handed down a reinterpretation of the Comstock Laws, allowing the public transport of "things which might intelligently be employed by conscientious and competent physicians for the purpose of saving life or promoting the well-being of their patients."

For Sanger, such triumph was bittersweet. Her movement had taken hold, but she could no longer determine its direction. She had always been a radical, even a zealot, who had proposed an idea and worked single-mindedly to promote it. But the people she'd convinced to join her movement did not always share her priorities or her commitment. That reality was underlined in 1942, five years after her official retirement due to poor health. The leadership of the organization was now mostly in the hands of men, who changed the name from the Birth Control Federation of America to the Planned Parenthood Federation of America.

Sanger's purpose had always been to give women the ability to control their lives by controlling their fertility. She believed the euphemistic emphasis on "parenthood" rather than on the sexual and reproductive life of women was enough to undermine the social and political significance of her mission. The change of name alienated Sanger from the organization and the movement she'd devoted her life to building. In 1966 (the same year I began my graduate studies in midwifery), Margaret Sanger died, having lived to see the birth of another of the twentieth century's most important movements—the women's equal rights movement.

Abortion Should Be a Civil Right

Betty Friedan

Betty Friedan is credited with launching the feminist movement with the publication of her book The Feminine Mystique. *In her book Friedan argues that long-held attitudes about gender subjugate women. The following selection was originally given as a speech to the 1969 national conference for the repeal of abortion laws. In it she asserts that abortion is central to sexual equality. She concludes that women's right to choose when and if to have children is vital to their achieving full human dignity and true equality with men. Friedan, who died in 2006, helped found the National Organization for Women, the National Abortion Rights Action League, and the National Women's Political Caucus. She was also the author of* It Changed My Life: Writings on the Women's Movement *and* The Fountain of Age.

Women, even though they're almost too visible as sex objects in this country, are invisible people. As the Negro was the invisible man, so women are the invisible people in America today: women who have a share in the decisions of the mainstream of government, of politics, of the church— who don't just cook the church supper, but preach the sermon; who don't just look up the ZIP codes and address the envelopes, but make the political decisions; who don't just do the housework of industry, but make some of the executive decisions. Women, above all, who say what their own lives and personalities are going to be, and no longer listen to or even permit male experts to define what 'feminine' is or isn't.

The essence of the denigration of women is our definition as sex object. To confront our inequality, therefore, we must

Betty Friedan, *Twentieth-Century Speeches*. New York: Penguin Books, 1992. Copyright © 1992 by Brian MacArthur. All rights reserved. Reproduced by permission of the author.

confront both society's denigration of us in these terms and our own self-denigration as people.

Motherhood Should Be a Choice

Am I saying that women must be liberated from sex? No. I am saying that sex will only be liberated to be a human dialogue, sex will only cease to be a sniggering, dirty joke and an obsession in this society, when women become active self-determining people, liberated to a creativity beyond motherhood, to a full human creativity.

Am I saying that women must be liberated from motherhood? No. I am saying that motherhood will only be a joyous and responsible human act when women are free to make, with full conscious choice and full human responsibility, the decisions to become mothers. Then, and only then, will they be able to embrace motherhood without conflict, when they will be able to define themselves not just as somebody's mother, not just as servants of children, not just as breeding receptacles, but as people for whom motherhood is a freely chosen part of life, freely celebrated while it lasts, but for whom creativity has many more dimensions, as it has for men.

Then, and only then, will motherhood cease to be a curse and a chain for men and for children. For despite all the lip service paid to motherhood today, all the roses sent on Mother's Day, all the commercials and the hypocritical ladies' magazines' celebration of women in their roles as housewives and mothers, the fact is that all television or night-club comics have to do is go before a microphone and say the words 'my wife,' and the whole audience erupts into gales of guilty, vicious and obscene laughter.

The hostility between the sexes has never been worse. The image of women in avant-garde plays, novels and movies, and behind the family situation comedies on television is that mothers are man-devouring, cannibalistic monsters, or else

Lolitas, sex objects—and objects not even of heterosexual impulse, but of sadomasochism. That impulse—the punishment of women—is much more of a factor in the abortion question than anybody ever admits.

Motherhood is a bane almost by definition, or at least partly so, as long as women are forced to be mothers—and only mothers—against their will. Like a cancer cell living its life through another cell, women today are forced to live too much through their children and husbands (they are too dependent on them, and therefore are forced to take too much varied resentment, vindictiveness, inexpressible resentment and rage out on their husbands and children).

Buried Resentment

Perhaps it is the least understood fact of American political life: the enormous buried violence of women in this country today. Like all oppressed people, women have been taking their violence out on their own bodies, in all the maladies with which they plague the MDs and the psychoanalysts. Inadvertently, and in subtle and insidious ways, they have been taking their violence out, too, on their children and on their husbands, and sometimes they're not so subtle.

The battered-child syndrome that we are hearing more and more about from our hospitals is almost always to be found in the instance of unwanted children, and women are doing the battering, as much or more than men. In the case histories of psychologically and physically maimed children, the woman is always the villain, and the reason is our definition of her: not only as passive sex object, but as mother, servant, someone else's mother, someone else's wife.

Am I saying that women have to be liberated from men? That men are the enemy? No. I am saying the *men* will only be truly liberated to love women and to be fully themselves when women are liberated to have a full say in the decisions of their lives and their society.

Until that happens, men are going to bear the guilty burden of the passive destiny they have forced upon women, the suppressed resentment, the sterility of love when it is not between two fully active, joyous people, but has in it the element of exploitation. And men will not be free to be all they can be as long as they must live up to an image of masculinity that disallows all the tenderness and sensitivity in a man, all that might be considered feminine. Men have enormous capacities in them that they have to repress and fear in order to live up to the obsolete, brutal, bear-killing, Ernest Hemingway, crew-cut Prussian, napalm-all-the-children-in-Vietnam, bang-bang-you're-dead image of masculinity. Men are not allowed to admit that they sometimes are afraid. They are not allowed to express their own sensitivity, their own need to be passive sometimes and not always active. Men are not allowed to cry. So they are only half-human, as women are only half-human, until we can go this next step forward. All the burdens and responsibilities that men are supposed to shoulder alone makes them, I think, resent women's pedestal, much as that pedestal may be a burden for women.

The Real Sexual Revolution

This is the real sexual revolution. Not the cheap headlines in the papers about at what age boys and girls go to bed with each other and whether they do it with or without the benefit of marriage. That's the least of it. The real sexual revolution is the emergence of women from passivity, from the point where they are the easiest victims for all the seductions, the waste, the worshiping of false gods in our affluent society, to full self-determination and full dignity. And it is the emergence of men from the stage where they are inadvertent brutes and masters to sensitive, complete humanity.

This revolution cannot happen without radical changes in the family as we know it today; in our concepts of marriage and love, in our architecture, our cities, our theology, our

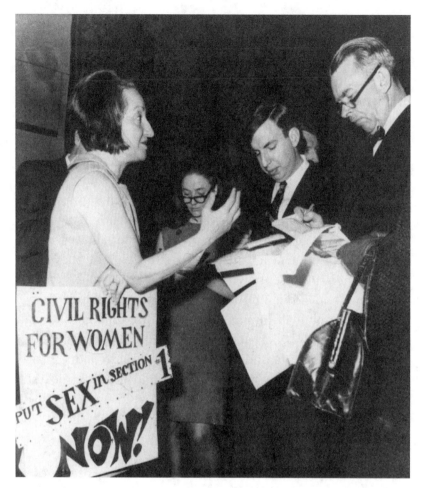

Betty Friedan, founder of the National Organization for Women, tells reporters that their organization intends to "put sex into section I" of the New York State constitution. Library of Congress

politics, our art. Not that women are special. Not that women are superior. But these expressions of human creativity are bound to be infinitely more various and enriching when women and men are allowed to relate to each other beyond the strict confines of the *Ladies' Home Journal*'s definition of the Mamma and Papa marriage.

If we are finally allowed to become full people, not only will children be born and brought up with more love and responsibility than today, but we will break out of the confines of that sterile little suburban family to relate to each other in terms of all of the possible dimensions of our personalities—male and female, as comrades, as colleagues, as friends, as lovers. And without so much hate and jealousy and buried resentment and hypocrisies, there will be a whole new sense of love that will make what we call love on Valentine's Day look very pallid.

Changing the Terms of the Abortion Debate

It's crucial, therefore, that we see this question of abortion as more than a quantitative move, more than a politically expedient move. Abortion repeal is not a question of political expediency. It is part of something greater. It is historic that we are addressing ourselves this weekend to perhaps the first national confrontation of women and men. Women's voices are finally being heard aloud, saying it the way it is about the question of abortion both in its most basic sense of morality and in its new political sense as part of the unfinished revolution of sexual equality.

In this confrontation, we are making an important milestone in this marvelous revolution that began long before any of us here were born and which still has a long way to go. As the pioneers from Mary Wollstonecraft to Margaret Sanger gave us the consciousness that brought us from our several directions here, so we here, in changing the very terms of the debate on abortion to assert woman's right to choose, and to define the terms of our lives ourselves, move women further to full human dignity. Today, we moved history forward.

The Evolution of the Pro-Life Movement

Jack Willke

Jack Willke, a physician and an ardent pro-life activist, recounts the history of the pro-life movement in the following selection. Willke and his wife, Barbara, were on the front lines of pro-life activism even before the Roe v. Wade *decision legalizing abortion was handed down by the Supreme Court. Willke describes the inner workings of many antiabortion organizations, including the National Right to Life Committee and the Christian Coalition. He concludes by saying that the pro-life movement has a long way to go, as evidenced by the fact that abortion is still legal. Willke, a physician and lecturer, is president of the International Right to Life Federation and the Life Issues Institute. He is also the author of* Handbook on Abortion *and* Abortion, Questions and Answers: Why Can't We Love Them Both?

In the early years (1967 through 1972), Colorado, California, and New York led the way in legalizing abortion. A dozen other smaller states also legalized abortion prior to the 1973 *Roe v. Wade* decision, but, in almost every case, these changes were highly restrictive. The activity in California and New York was obviously most important.

At that time, the leaders of the movement included: Professor Robert Byrn from Fordham University; Dr. Eugene Diamond and Dennis Horan from Chicago; Joseph Whitherspoon in Texas; Dr. Matthew Bulfin in Florida; and Dr. Joseph Stanton in Massachusetts. These were a few of the very early pioneers. They wrote, lectured, and helped to get the pro-life engine started.

Jack Willke, *Back to the Drawing Board: The Future of the Pro-Life Movement.* South Bend, IN: St. Augustine's Press, 2003. Copyright © 2003 by Teresa R. Wagner. All rights reserved. Reproduced by permission.

Organizationally, the Knights of Columbus, a Catholic fraternal and insurance group, warrant special mention. With approximately a million members, they were able to publish and circulate educational literature as no other organization could. Their many local branches provided invaluable ground troops at the start.

In 1971 and 1972, Mrs. Willke and I published the *Handbook on Abortion* and the *Life or Death* brochure, respectively. These were the first two universally distributed, major educational pieces. They provided the margin of victory for the referenda victories in North Dakota and Michigan in the fall of 1972. (These measures would have legalized abortion up to twenty weeks. The referendum in North Dakota was defeated by 78 percent, the one in Michigan by 63 percent.)

Then Came *Roe*

Before the dust of the January 1973 *Roe v. Wade* decision had settled, a number of us met to examine the arguments that had proven convincing to the U.S. Supreme Court. There were two major ones. First and most central was the Court's refusal to recognize prenatal life as fully human life. This was not a baby—at least not yet—to the Court. Second was the finding that abortion was only a religious issue. In 1973, this meant the issue was "Catholic," which meant, in turn, imposed by the American Catholic Bishops.

To address the first finding of the Court, we devised a methodology of teaching the pro-life story. It was quite simple. First, using slides of fetal development, we presented the scientific case that human life began at fertilization. We then explained that the issue was broader than religious belief; it was, in fact, a matter of human rights. We noted the comparison with slavery and the then-current drive for passing civil rights legislation to give equal status in the U.S. to people of color. Since the racial human rights issue could be addressed by corrective legislation, we argued that the fetal human rights issue could as well.

One early worry concerned the limited time-frame during which we thought *Roe* had to be reversed. As the number of abortions rose to 1.5 million annually, so did the number of individuals with a vested interest in justifying abortion and maintaining its legal status. Each pregnant woman involves a man, and the woman seeking an abortion typically consults two other people in her abortion decision: a mother, a sister, a girlfriend, etc. Thus, four times 1.5 million would equal 6 million people a year added to the roster of those with an interest in legal abortion. In ten years, that number could reach 60 million people—almost as many as vote in a general election.

But now, after thirty years [in 2003], we can look back and see that we had some, but certainly not an overwhelming, reason to be worried. We assumed that the great majority of those involved in abortion would be partisan supporters of it. Instead, their *silence* has been deafening. Men and women have suffered, not benefited, by abortion, with both psychological devastation and physical injury. We have seen that abortion contains within itself the seeds of its own destruction. To our surprise and delight, we are now seeing a generation of young people who have only known legal abortion in their lifetimes, but who are now providing strong leadership to stop it some day.

Even so, *abortion* has infected everything it has touched. Our entire culture has been changed.

Activism in the 1980s

As we approached the '80s, things really began to happen. The first major legislative accomplishment was the Hyde Amendment (1976), which stopped federal funding of elective abortions. Congressman Henry Hyde (R-IL) became a hero of the movement and remains so. We could name many in the U.S.

House and Senate who deserve the title of heroic leadership, but let's pick out three pioneers: In addition to Congressman Hyde is Congressman Chris Smith of New Jersey, and Senator Jesse Helms of North Carolina. These three men were rock solid, never deviated from the pro-life movement and have simply been invaluable.

The year 1980 was a milestone. First, Ronald Reagan was elected President, which meant that pro-life leaders worked both with and within the administration. Reverend Jerry Falwell of the Moral Majority became a national figure with the help and influence of Paul Weyrich, an important and influential conservative and pro-lifer.

In evangelical circles, two figures came to the fore: Francis Schaeffer, a Protestant theologian, and Dr. C. Everett Koop, then of the Children's Hospital in Philadelphia and later President Reagan's Surgeon General. Both wrote and lectured around the country with a stirring message. They warned that the country was losing its Christian moorings and that Christians should therefore come out of their churches and participate in political and public life. They encouraged evangelicals to work with other pro-lifers, especially Roman Catholics and members of other faiths. Evangelicals responded, becoming a major political force, giving rise to the Christian Coalition and other activist groups.

One excellent example of evangelical influence and industry is the National Religious Broadcasters network. Overseas observers are astonished to find out that the almost 2,000 evangelical stations in the United States are, without exception, 100 percent pro-life. These stations have 60 million or more listeners every week and are a major reason why the pro-abortion media conglomerates in the U.S. have not completely dominated and changed the culture here. Individuals such as the Reverend T. James Kennedy of Coral Ridge Ministries, Marlin Maddoux of Point of View, Chuck Colson of Prison Fellowship, and of course Dr. James Dobson of Focus on the Family, are just a few of the radio personalities who have inspired pro-life activism. Dr. Dobson, in particular, is a modern phenomenon. Without question, he is the most significant, most respected, and most influential evangelical spokesperson in the United States—perhaps even in the world. His position is 100 percent pro-life, his approach is totally professional, and his impact on our culture has been simply beyond measuring.

Organized Groups Emerge

At the same time, Mrs. Phyllis Schlafly rose to prominence by founding the Eagle Forum and almost single-handedly defeated the Equal Rights Amendment (proposed in 1972 and finally buried in 1987), which would have inserted abortion-on-demand into the Constitution as an amendment, rather than by the Supreme Court decision of *Roe v. Wade.*

In the District of Columbia, other pro-life, activist groups were forming, including the Christian Action Council, the Ad-Hoc Committee in Defense of Life, and the March for Life. Americans United for Life, a pro-life public-interest law firm, had begun in Chicago and was a major player, as was the National Right to Life Committee, which had been formed in 1973 and was where I served as President, 1980–1991.

In the 1970s, the aforementioned organizations were more or less co-equal. During the 1980s, however, the National Right to Life Committee [NRLC] became dominant. From 1980 to 1991, it grew from five to fifty employees, and went from $400,000 annual cash flow to $15 million. With its fifty state affiliates, it was clearly the leading pro-life force.

Happily, other groups arose, grew, and prospered. They matured alongside NRLC to a co-equal status, so that now there are a number of major national organizations fluctuating in terms of specific leadership. Gary Bauer, President of the Family Research Council from 1980–1998, became the prime pro-life spokesman in the Nation's Capital during the

1990s, for example. The Christian Coalition had spokesman Ralph Reed; Concerned Women for America was led by Beverly LaHaye (and now Sandy Rios). Richard Land's Southern Baptist's Christian Life Commission as well as Phyllis Schlafly's Eagle Forum have become significant players in Washington politics, along with the more recent Christian Medical Association under Dr. Dave Stephens. The United States Catholic Conference, also in D.C., has always been a strong and influential pro-life presence. . . .

Failures

Let us now review both the failures and successes.

First, of course, we have failed to stop abortion. The roadblock, obviously, is the U.S. Supreme Court, which has permitted legislation in limited areas, which we have used (parental involvement laws, informed consent provisions, etc.). But abortion continues.

We have lost the National Democrat Party leadership. While incremental over the years, this development is now undeniable and unfortunate.

We have not influenced the secular media. Publications such as the *New York Times*, the *Washington Post*, along with all the major networks have been bulwarks for the abortion movement from the beginning, and remain so.

We have not been able to penetrate the near unanimous Jewish support of abortion-on-demand (recognizing, of course, that Orthodox Jewry, a very small minority, is strongly pro-life).

We have not been able to affect the pro-abortion policies of many of the mainline Protestant churches, though these policies are weakening by themselves in churches like the United Methodist and the Presbyterian Church U.S.A. Significantly, these Protestant churches are seeing rapidly declining membership, as contrasted with the growth of the Southern

Baptists and of other evangelical and fundamentalist churches that are pro-life.

We have failed to penetrate the African American leadership in the U.S. Without question, polls show most black Americans as consistently more pro-life than whites. Nevertheless, their leadership, with very few exceptions, remains aggressively pro-abortion.

Leadership quarrels of the early 1980s set us back. Happily, those days are long gone, and the top leadership of all of the organizations now routinely work together warmly.

We failed to convince pastors and clergymen to preach aggressively against abortion.

Finally, we have failed to counter, adequately, the one remaining argument of the abortion lobby: That a woman has a *right* to choose.

Successes

We can be proud of what we have done right, however:

Abortion remains *the* central social issue of our time—even after thirty years.

Abortion in the U.S. is still a dirty word. An abortionist in the U.S. is still an outcast, especially within the medical profession. This is not true in many other nations, and it is an important deterrent to abortion in this country.

Few U.S. hospitals still do abortions, which are largely confined to freestanding facilities staffed by abortionists, who are, again, not part of the respected medical community.

Is this a baby? This is no longer a question. Ultrasound and other medical advances have been incredibly important in this, but the pro-life movement was of central importance in teaching the nation, beyond any question of scientific doubt, that human life begins at fertilization.

The pro-life movement has changed the way religious groups view each other and has encouraged them to work together. The prejudice and bigotry that divided denominations,

Christian and other, are gone, as any sidewalk counselor will attest. We've learned and lived the old saw, "If you don't hang together, you'll end up hanging separately."

Our religious radio, a shining triumph in the U.S., is the envy of pro-life movements around the world. This industry is totally pro-life.

Our movement has not just survived, but grown in the face of a militant, dedicated, and powerful pro-abortion media and academia. It has grown, too, in spite of the much greater financial resources of the abortion industry.

The U.S. has developed far and away the largest, best-organized and most effective pro-life movement in the international arena.

Most Americans are still opposed to most abortions done in this country. *Roe* and its progeny created a policy and practice of abortion-on-demand that remain radically far from the wishes and convictions of the average American citizen, who would permit it only for three months, and only for a fairly narrow set of circumstances.

We have refuted most of the arguments of the abortion lobby. Space doesn't permit, but their myths include: back-alley abortions; unwanted pregnancy equals unwanted child and child abuse; it's only a religious issue; we need it to control overpopulation; rape pregnancies are common and must be aborted; and fetal handicap is an absolute indication for abortion.

We have had prominent converts to the cause, including Dr. Bernard Nathanson, founding member of the National Abortion and Reproductive Rights Action League (NARRAL), and Norma McCorvey, the "Roe" of *Roe v. Wade*. They have become important leaders in the movement.

Finally, young people are a vigorous component of the movement. They are addressing not just abortion but also teen abstinence, a movement that, if it continues, will have a major impact.

The Future

There are many question marks.

The battle over abortion is slowly being won, but it is tied closely to the issue of family life. We have seen in the last several decades the deterioration and fragmentation of the family. Divorce is rampant, pre-marital co-habitation is common, illegitimacy, in some areas, is almost the norm. In the last few years we've seen hopeful signs of this beginning to plateau and, in some cases, turn around. It is difficult to imagine that we could effectively stop abortion unless we first return more stability to family life.

Pornography is a related issue. It is out of control and is terribly damaging.

Bioethical questions, with new ones arising every month, will influence the direction of the movement. Today we kill babies *inside* the womb to get her unpregnant. Tomorrow will we be killing babies *outside* of the womb, and again for choice?

What influence will the web have? Certainly it will be profound, for good or for evil.

And now demographics, to many people's surprise, enters the world stage with an unexpected impact: Overpopulation will soon become underpopulation, with nations aggressively campaigning for more babies rather than fewer.

In the end, it will be the commitment and dedication of those within the pro-life movement that carry the day. Their devotion and perseverance are far beyond those within the pro-abortion movement. Without the media, the government and money, the pro-abortion movement collapses. Their strength is a mile wide but only a yard deep.

Leadership during the 1970s was often lonely. More than once, Barbara [Willke] and I and others wondered if a mutual disaster took us out, would the pro-life movement continue? But today its base is broad, dedicated, and informed. If one leader or organization stumbles, others pick up the flag and charge on. This movement will not go away.

Finally, while religious belief and practice are not *the* reason to oppose abortion in this secular nation, these factors are prime motivators. As this nation slowly returns to its religious base, the high number of God-fearing, ordinary citizens will yet turn this thing around.

I may not live to see the end of abortion, but I am convinced my children will.

Violence at Abortion Clinics

Patricia Baird-Windle and Eleanor J. Bader

When peaceful methods for stopping abortion were not success-
ful, some antiabortionists resorted to violence. The first arson at
an abortion clinic occurred in 1977, and by 1983 acts of violence
numbered in the hundreds at clinics throughout the United
States. In the following selection Patricia Baird-Windle and
Eleanor J. Bader recount several incidents of arson and a kid-
napping of an abortion doctor and his wife. The authors note
that clinic operators received little help from law enforcement
during these events. Baird-Windle was an abortion provider for
twenty-three years and is one of the founders of the National
Coalition of Abortion Providers. Bader is a social worker and
political journalist.

When evangelical Christians Dr. C. Everett Koop and Francis Schaeffer began touring the country with their book and film, *What Ever Happened to the Human Race?*, they warned the thousands who came to see them that *Roe v. Wade* [which legalized abortion] symbolized the triumph of evil over good. It was 1979. Virtue could surely trump sin, they added, but only if Christian activists committed themselves to selfless organizing and relentless activism. Luckily for them, the Moral Majority had just formed and founder Jerry Falwell promised that he would register at least four million conservative Christian voters before the 1980 elections. Pundits everywhere declared the first rumblings of a culture war and anticipated many heady moments for born-again right-wingers.

Indeed, Ronald Reagan's 1980 victory over Jimmy Carter was attributed to the influx of evangelical voters. While nonfundamentalist constituencies panicked at the number of reli-

Patricia Baird-Windle and Eleanor J. Bader, *Targets of Hatred: Anti-Abortion Terrorism.* New York: Palgrave, 2001. Copyright © 2001 by Patricia Baird-Windle and Eleanor J. Bader. All rights reserved. Reproduced by permission.

gious traditionalists who had gained power on both the federal and local levels, Protestant conservatives recognized that for the first time in nearly a decade, reversing *Roe v. Wade*—and undoing other gains of the 1960s and 1970s—were real possibilities. Joseph Scheidler [founder of the Pro-Life Action League] had a public, photographed meeting with the president in the first months of the Reagan administration. Furthermore, the appointment of C. Everett Koop as surgeon general invigorated the movement. It seemed only a matter of time before the law shifted in a right-wing direction.

But the euphoria—at least as far as abortion was concerned—was short-lived. In 1981 two different bills came before Congress, and disagreement over which to support led to splits between pro-life forces. On one side, Catholic bishops were endorsing a Human Life Amendment [HLA] that would have nullified *Roe*. Conversely, the New Right was putting its energy into a Human Life Bill (HLB). Convinced that the amendment was a pie-in-the-sky effort, a panoply of newly organized groups felt that the HLB was more realistic since it would permanently prohibit taxpayer-funded abortions and remove federal court jurisdiction in overturning state anti-abortion measures. Despite its more incremental approach, when the HLB came up for a vote it was defeated; shortly thereafter, Senator Orrin Hatch [R-UT], sponsor of the HLA, withdrew the bill from consideration, presumably to avoid a second loss.

Conservatives Were Concerned

Conservatives were perplexed by the bills' thwarting. In addition, they had other cause for concern. Reagan's appointment of Sandra Day O'Connor to the United States Supreme Court in September 1981 shocked anti-abortionists who believed that her opposition to reproductive choice was insufficiently ironclad.

There was also the issue of culture. Music Television (MTV) debuted in 1981, attracting scores of teenagers and young adults to the irreverent words and music of The Cure, Madonna, NWA, Public Enemy and REM. U2's "Sunday Bloody Sunday" had become an antiwar anthem in 1983, and Bruce Springsteen's "Born in the USA," a Vietnam veteran's lament that was released in 1984, was keeping America's aggressive foreign policy in public view. Even pop star Michael Jackson, whose "Thriller" topped the charts during the early 1980s, seemed to celebrate androgyny and bend definitions of male and female.

While the United States poured millions of dollars into support for international right-wing movements and made some headway in defeating progressive movements in Africa and Central America, the domestic agenda that had originally attracted so many people to the conservative cause was floundering. Paul Laxalt's [R-NV] "Family Protection Act," a thirty-five-point conservative wish list for domestic policy, never made it to the floor of Congress, deemed too much too soon by even the most ideologically supportive. Meanwhile, Gay Pride parades were becoming annual events and queer and feminist publications were proliferating throughout North America.

Small wonder, then, that many zealous ideologues felt betrayed. After years of quiet fortitude, they began formulating direct-action strategies for ending abortion, affirmative action, pornography and lesbian and gay equality. According to reporters James Risen and Judy L. Thomas, between January 1983 and March 1985 at least 319 acts of violence were committed against 238 reproductive health centers. (This estimate is undoubtedly low; clinics are often loath to burden themselves with reporting anti-abortion incidents since police rarely do anything to help them.) In fact, as early as 1982, clinic fire-bombings, picket lines and equipment sabotage were regularly featured on the evening news.

Still, when three men calling themselves the Army of God kidnapped clinic owner Dr. Hector Zevallos and his wife, Rosalee Jean, in August 1982, both providers and the pro-choice community understood that the terrain had shifted. A new era in which activists would stop at nothing to win the fight against abortion—and by extension attempt to limit women's autonomy—had begun. . . .

Clinic Is Gutted by Fire

The day after the ninth anniversary of *Roe v. Wade*, the Hope Clinic for Women was gutted by fire. "It happened late on a Saturday night so no one was hurt, but one-third of the building was destroyed," says Allison Hile, on staff since 1979. "Nobody was caught. In 1982 you didn't call BATF [Bureau of Alcohol, Tobacco, and Firearms] or the FBI. You called the local police; when we did, they told us they didn't deal with abortion clinics."

Police recalcitrance notwithstanding, the staff decided that their collective elbow grease and dedication would be enough to get the clinic back in operation. "The night of the fire the executive director got a phone tree going to the staff. We got a generator in for light and the whole staff spent Sunday and Monday cleaning up," says Hile. "On Tuesday we saw patients. The building we were in was owned by Dr. Hector Zevallos. He had his private practice in one part of the building and the clinic took up the other part. We used the waiting area of his private practice to see patients for the six weeks it took us to rebuild."

Hile credits the fire with changing the behavior of local anti-abortionists who had been tormenting the clinic since it opened in 1974. "Some of the regulars were embarrassed by the people in their movement who would try to burn a building," she says. "That feeling has lasted to this day." In addition, a well-enforced injunction bars the blockading of clinic doors and has been an effective deterrent during vigils and demonstrations.

An Abortion Doctor Is Kidnapped

Dr. Hector Zevallos had owned the Hope Clinic for Women for eight years when he and his wife, Rosalee Jean, were kidnapped from their home in the summer of 1982. The evening had started out fairly typically. Mrs. Zevallos was watching TV and her husband was puttering in another part of the house when three men knocked on the door and asked to see a piece of property that the Zevalloses were selling. When Hector went outside to show them the lot, one of the kidnappers pulled a gun on him. The men then got Rosalee Jean, blindfolded the pair, and threw them into a car.

"This happened on a Thursday," says Allison Hile, at that time a clinic counselor. "Friday morning, the thirteenth, it looked like Hector was late for work. It was odd since he always arrived promptly to get ready." When Hector had not shown up by midmorning, clinic workers called his home. Since no one answered, they called a neighbor and had her check on him. "His door was open, the TV was on, and the bowl of popcorn was on the table. She said it was really eerie," says Hile. "We called the police because we knew he was missing. We had other doctors, but by Saturday we were getting more and more concerned. To make matters worse, the executive director, Laura Moody, was also suddenly gone from the clinic, dealing with the police and the FBI. She was stationed at the Zevallos's home, which became police headquarters during the search."

When the Zevallos's eight-day ordeal was over, Hile, other staff, and a concerned public learned what had happened. The kidnappers, mastermind Don Benny Anderson and teenage brothers Matthew and Wayne Moore, had ordered Dr. Zevallos to make an audiotape intended to convince then President Reagan to make abortion illegal. Both Hector and Rosalee remained blindfolded during their entire captivity; their kidnappers also made them sleep on the frigid cement floor of an abandoned National Guard munitions bunker, fed them cold sandwiches, and did not allow them to bathe or use conventional toilet facilities.

"Hector finally made the anti-abortion tape at gunpoint," says Hile. But the three, calling themselves the Army of God, were still not satisfied and began to pester the doctor to close his clinic. "For seven days and nights he discussed the issue with them, but he would not agree to close the office. The last night things got a lot worse, and he and Rosalee were treated more harshly than they had been treated before," says Hile. "Dr. Zevallos asked them why this was and one of the Moore brothers said he'd been up all night trying to formulate a plan to kill the doctor but still didn't know how to do it. That night Mrs. Zevallos was grabbed, physically assaulted for the first time. At that point Hector said he would close the clinic but needed to go free so that he could talk to his partners about the decision. The kidnappers agreed to let them go and drove Dr. and Mrs. Zevallos to a hill near their home. When they walked into their house, a million people were there and they were confused, disoriented."

"I remember being scared at two particular points," recalls Hile, "When the receiving doorbell at the clinic would ring, if it was a small package being delivered, we were terrified. We imagined Hector's hand or a finger being sent by the kidnappers. The other time I got scared I was at home, in the yard with my husband. I didn't know what was going on and it all caught up with me."

During Dr. Zevallos's absence and for several weeks after his return, the clinic's counseling director brought therapists in to run support groups for those workers desiring help. "We'd sit in the recovery room at the end of each day sharing our worst fears and digging our heels in," says Hile.

Effects of Kidnapping Spread Widely

While everyone connected with the Hope Clinic was tremendously shaken by the kidnapping, providers across the country were also adversely impacted by it. "I remember hearing about the kidnapping and thinking it was a bad joke," says Susan Hill, president of the National Women's Health Organization. "None of us had ever heard of the Army of God, and none of us had expected things to move from damaging property to hurting us personally. The kidnapping was the first time providers as a group understood the personal threat we faced. The doctors who worked for the National Women's Health Organization started to call and would ask me to reassure them and their families that they were safe. We had ten clinics at that point and I tried to assure people, but I couldn't promise them that they'd be okay. In retrospect, the kidnapping represents the first attack on the supply of doctors. Because the Reagan administration didn't talk to us, in most places we were on our own. We had to add security ourselves. In cities like Fargo and Ft. Wayne—where the antis had been very visible and disruptive—we had to convince doctors to fly in from four states away. It was like a ripple effect. Dr. Zevallos was kidnapped, then there was a fire someplace, and then a bombing. You could not relax since there was always a reminder that they—the antis—were out there. The kidnapping, 1982, marks the time when all providers started to be on twenty-four-hour alert."

Follow-up note: Police caught Anderson and the Moore brothers after Dr. Zevallos provided police with a detailed account of the route they had driven to get to the abandoned concrete ammunition bunker where he and Rosalee were detained. Surprisingly, despite being blindfolded, Zevallos was able to recall the turns the car had taken. This provided the police with the data they needed to apprehend the kidnappers.

Don Benny Anderson was sentenced to two thirty-year terms in prison. Matthew and Wayne Moore each received extended prison terms. Although Dr. Zevallos retired in 1986, at the age of fifty-seven, he still owns the Hope Clinic for Women. He and Rosalee Jean divorced a year after the incident. . . .

Another Clinic Is Torched

Staff at the Feminist Women's Health Center (FWHC) in Yakima, Washington, open since 1980, were so pleased with the work they were doing that, in late 1982, they decided to expand their services and open a second clinic in Everett, three hours away. They were completely unprepared for the hostile reception that greeted them. "As soon as the antis heard we were opening they came en masse," says staffer Beverly Whipple. "There was a daily onslaught. Something was always happening. We'd get hundreds of phone calls—seven hundred hangups in one day—which effectively blocked our phone lines. It was impossible to get any work done."

According to Whipple, the antis would also fill every parking space adjacent to the clinic and cover workers' cars with pictures of dismembered fetuses. Individual demonstrators would then form a gauntlet for patients to walk through. They trespassed, followed staff home at night, and copied down the license numbers of incoming patients. "The building was surrounded by ivy, and they'd crawl through the plants to look into our windows," she adds. "They took still photos and videotapes of patients and on November 19 held a prayer vigil in front of the clinic. The protestors had received permission from the City Council to block the road for this event; they had a flatbed truck and a complete sound system and brought hundreds of people to the facility to pray for us."

Two and a half weeks later, on December 3, a man subsequently identified as Curtis Beseda tossed gasoline into a clinic window and ignited it. "The fire did significant damage, destroying a lot of equipment," says Whipple. "But when the fire inspectors came, they suggested that we'd set it ourselves.

They said that since we weren't doing well financially, and were a new business under a lot of pressure, perhaps the fire had been our doing. The fire marshal wanted to investigate the staff. We tried to point out how ludicrous this was, but they would not even speak to the antis until we were investigated and came out clean. They wanted us to take lie detector tests. Our attorney said that he understood our refusal, but that if we wanted the case to move forward we had to do the polygraphs. We all took the test and we all, inexplicably, flunked. They eventually threw the test results out and started to question the antis."

A Second and Third Fire

The clinic remained closed for two months, until February 1, 1984. That month, and for most of March, it was picketed every day and received an enormous volume of hate mail. Then, on March 26, a second fire was set. This time the clinic had better security and the fire was quickly extinguished. "The gasoline was poured into a counseling room and lit, but the damage affected only one room so we were able to close it off, clear out the smoke, and open later that day. After this fire the officials started to investigate the antis more seriously. Regional BATF had never been involved in a clinic fire in this state before and they were called in," Whipple says.

At the time of the second fire, the clinic was in court seeking an injunction to stop the antis from trespassing and harassing patients and staff. A trial to address this request began on April 19; on the night of April 20, a third fire broke out at the FWHC and caused extensive damage not only to the clinic but also to the building that housed it.

The Everett FWHC never reopened. Although Whipple says that for years staff held onto the hope that they would be able to resurrect the center, financial pressures coupled with an inhospitable community made this impossible.

According to a history of the clinic written in 1996, "Months after the third fire, local police questioned, but chose not to prosecute, Curtis Beseda. However, federal authorities took the violence more seriously and it paid off. Beseda fled to Canada and federal Marshals arrested him when he tried to re-enter the United States. On the witness stand, Beseda admitted he set the three fires in Everett and another in Bellingham. He was sentenced to 20 years."

Follow-up note: In February 1986 the FWHC filed a federal civil lawsuit charging individual protestors with violating the Racketeer Influenced Corrupt Organizations (RICO) Act. Several of the defendants settled out of court, and their payment made it possible for the Yakima health center to purchase the building they currently occupy. A 1990 trial on the RICO claims resulted in another victory for the FWHC and three defendants, Curtis Beseda, Sharon Codispoti and Dotti Roberts, were ordered to pay more than $300,000 to the clinic. Not surprisingly, they appealed the decision. The case was subsequently assigned to a three-judge panel; FWHC staffers were perplexed that one of the judicial panelists had previously been a National Right to Life Committee board member. In August 1995, nearly five years after the appeal was initiated, the panel reversed the lower court decision and ordered the FWHC to pay $19,058 in defendants' court costs. They had no choice but to do so.

Curtis Beseda was released on October 3, 1996 after serving twelve years in prison.

Over the last two decades, North Dakota and Florida police and BATF officers have repeated the slur first uttered in Everett, suggesting that clinic owners or staff were responsible for fires started at clinics in these states. The evidence reveals the lie embedded in this scurrilous assertion; no owner or worker has ever been found guilty of arson.

Operation Rescue and Civil Disobedience

Faye Ginsburg

The pro-life movement has three factions. At one end of the spectrum are those who try to outlaw abortion mainly through legislative efforts; on the other end are violent activists who burn clinics and murder abortion providers. Somewhere in the middle is Operation Rescue. In the following selection Faye Ginsburg examines Operation Rescue, a group whose tactics include massive demonstrations, or "rescues," designed to disrupt activities at abortion clinics. Ginsburg discusses how Randall Terry, the founder of Operation Rescue, was a skilled organizer and recruiter who garnered national media attention and publicity for his group. Even though Operation Rescue is not as active today as it was in the late 1980s and early 1990s, Ginsburg concludes that Terry's efforts had a profound and lasting effect on the pro-life movement. Ginsburg is a professor of anthropology at New York University. She is the author of Contested Lives: The Abortion Debate in an American Community *and* Conceiving the New World Order: The Global Politics of Reproduction.

At six o'clock in the morning on 28 November 1987, Randall Terry, a lanky, twenty-seven-year-old born-again Christian from upstate New York, led his first official "rescue," a blockade of an abortion clinic in Cherry Hill, New Jersey. Three hundred rescuers sealed off access to the building. As Terry describes it, "We sang, prayed, read psalms," and conducted a parachurch service "on the doorstep of hell for nearly eleven hours! No babies died. It was glorious, peaceful, and

Faye Ginsburg, "Rescuing the Nation," *Abortion Wars: A Half Century of Struggle, 1950-2000.* Berkeley: University of California Press, 1998. Originally published in *Fundamentalisms and the State: Remaking Polities, Economies, and Militance,* edited by Martin E. Marty and R. Scott Appleby, Chicago: University of Chicago Press. Copyright © 1993 by The University of Chicago. All rights reserved. Reproduced by permission.

prayerful." By the end of the day, 211 "mothers, fathers, grandmothers, grandfathers, and singles" had been arrested, charged with trespassing, and released.

Operation Rescue

The event served as the trial demonstration of a militant anti-abortion organization, Operation Rescue, composed of fundamentalist and evangelical Christians. The group was formally established in the spring of 1988 by Randall Terry and quickly escalated its activities. By 1989, Operation Rescue had gained a prominent, if notorious, reputation, even among fellow travelers in the pro-life movement. By 1990, according to the group's figures, there had been over thirty-five thousand arrests, while sixteen thousand individuals had risked arrest in what they call "rescues." Unlike those allied with other anti-abortion groups, which hold regular meetings, call upon political representatives, and in other ways operate as ongoing arenas of action, Operation Rescue relies on the existing infrastructure of independent fundamentalist churches and conservative Roman Catholic congregations and organizations as its base. For most members beyond the leadership, sporadic participation in "rescue" demonstrations constitutes the central activity. Focusing organizational energy into "rescues" takes maximum advantage of the publicity generated by dramatic confrontation.

The blockades carried out by Operation Rescue have been described variously as acts of "biblical obedience," civil disobedience, harassment, and terrorism, and even as a form of racketeering and antitrust action. The distinct positions represented by these terms suggest the complex and often ironic impact of this group.

Whatever the judgment of a particular observer, however, Operation Rescue's political tactics and philosophy distinguish it in two ways. First, it is the most confrontational and right-wing of the contemporary anti-abortion groups. Contrary to stereotypes that portray right-to-life activists as homogeneous and puritanical, a remnant of Victorian mores and family forms, the pro-life cause has generally tolerated a spectrum of practice, belief, and lifestyle through an overall commitment to moderation and single-issue politics. However, Operation Rescue's scorn for civil political process, its uncompromising interventionist tactics, and its absolutist Christian ideology have strained the alliances in the movement. For a decade after the 1973 *Roe v. Wade* decision legalizing abortion, right-to-life activism tended to take a civil approach, attempting to influence political action by working within the legislative and electoral systems. Since 1983, radical elements in the pro-life movement—from the Pro-Life Action League of ex-Benedectine monk Joseph Scheidler (whose work influenced Randall Terry) to individuals responsible for incidents of bombing and arson at abortion clinics—have become increasingly active and more visible than the moderate mainstream represented by the National Right to Life Committee. By the end of the 1980s, Operation Rescue had become the umbrella sheltering the more extreme activists.

Attracting Protestants and Catholics

As a second distinction, Operation Rescue is the first pro-life group not only to draw large numbers of conservative Protestants into ongoing, organized anti-abortion activity, but also to join them in action with conservative Roman Catholics. Terry himself has been heavily influenced by the teachings of the late evangelical Protestant, author Francis Schaeffer, who viewed legal abortion as the epitome of twentieth-century decadence. In his book, *A Christian Manifesto*, published in 1981, Schaeffer recommended civil disobedience in opposition to abortion as a way for evangelicals to "challenge the entire legitimacy of the secular modern state, withholding allegiance until the nation returns to its religious roots in matters like public prayer and religious education." It is not surprising, then, that Terry judged an event like Cherry Hill as a turning point not only because of its impact on abortion politics but also because of the response it generated in the Christian community. In this view, opposition to abortion is not the end so much as the means to a larger goal of returning America to "traditional Christian values." Terry has made this point with a combination of pastoral, industrial, religious, and military metaphors. "God is using us to separate sheep from goats . . . the wheat from the chaff," he writes. "There are a lot of people who believe this is going to be the seedbed of revival in the church, the locomotive to bring reformation in our culture. When the Lord put the vision in my heart, it was not just to rescue babies and mothers but to rescue the country. This is the first domino to fall."

Operation Rescue has catalyzed fundamentalist and evangelical participation in political action that began in America in the mid-1970s, bringing thousands of conservative Christians into the anti-abortion movement and transforming them in the process. In addition to expanding the revival of fundamentalist and evangelical social action, Operation Rescue has had a number of ironic consequences. For example, it has unintentionally served as one stimulus for reinvigorating the organization and focus of the pro-choice movement. It has also introduced a new element of dissension within the right-to-life movement, pushing activism in a more confrontational and militant direction. Like an impatient and unruly youngster (only "born" in 1988), Operation Rescue has disturbed the more settled, mature, and moderate anti-abortion veterans who have been organizing for twenty years.

NARAL Advocates Pregnancy Prevention

Karen S. Cooper

The abortion-rights group NARAL was founded in 1969 as the National Association for the Repeal of Abortion Laws. After the 1973 Roe v. Wade *Supreme Court decision legalizing abortion, the group changed the words of its acronym to National Abortion and Reproductive Rights Action League. It has since undergone another identity change and is now known as NARAL Pro-Choice America. In the following selection Karen C. Cooper describes how NARAL focuses on preventing unwanted pregnancies to reduce the need for abortions. She contends that practical methods such as sex education, birth control, and emergency contraception are far more effective in preventing unintended pregnancies than is a policy of abstinence only, which is promoted by antichoice groups. Cooper is the executive director for NARAL Pro-Choice Washington.*

With the 32nd anniversary of the *Roe v. Wade* decision this Saturday [Jan. 22, 2005], I reflect on the futures of my granddaughters with great concern. We know from the days before *Roe*, when countless women died from illegal abortions every year, that outlawing abortion doesn't stop it from happening.

Most people can agree that the best way to prevent abortions is to give women practical methods for preventing unintended pregnancies, such as comprehensive sex education, birth control and emergency contraception. Yet pro-life activists and politicians consistently oppose such policies.

Anti-choice leaders are the greatest obstacle to sensible policies that could help prevent unintended pregnancies and

Karen S. Cooper, "Sensible Policies Best Pregnancy Prevention," *Seattle Post-Intelligencer,* January 20, 2005, p. B7. Copyright © 2005 by Hearst Communications, Inc., Hearst Newspapers Division. Reproduced by permission.

abortion. The abstinence-only-until-marriage model that anti-choice leaders advocate is actually a call to return to the 1950s when women married at 18 to 20 years old. This is not a model for the 21st century, when half of the students in law school and medical school are women.

It is the pro-choice organizations and pro-choice elected officials who promote policies to prevent unintended pregnancies. NARAL Pro-Choice Washington actively has promoted responsible, comprehensive sex education programs. We have advocated for access to emergency contraception (the morning-after pill) through local pharmacies and in the emergency room for victims of sexual assault. Pro-choice organizations have worked to increase access to birth control by requiring insurance companies that cover prescription drugs to cover birth control pills.

In contrast, anti-choice groups and politicians strongly support using federal funding for abstinence-only-until-marriage sex education programs, which contain ideologically driven, medically inaccurate information. One such program is the WAIT Training, which lists "Financial Support" as one of the "5 Major Needs of Women," and "Domestic Support" as one of the "5 Major Needs of Men." They are teaching children that women should stay home and keep house while men go out and earn money.

Abstinence Is Unrealistic

In 1953, the average age of first marriage for women was 20; by 2003 the average age of first marriage for women had risen to 25. In 1970, 42 percent of first-time brides were teenagers; by 1990 just 17 percent of first-time brides were teenagers. Most of us consider this progress; we recognize that women are marrying later because they are completing college and often graduate school first. We also understand that better-educated women (like men) are far less likely to live in poverty.

Do any of us really think that young people will remain totally abstinent until their mid to late 20s when they finish college or graduate school? Of course not. The abstinence-only-until-marriage model that anti-choice leaders and politicians advocate doesn't make sense in today's world where the average age of first marriage is 25.

[In 2004,] there was a bill before Congress, the Putting Prevention First Act, which was co-sponsored by both of Washington's pro-choice senators, Maria Cantwell and Patty Murray. The bill would have funded health centers providing contraception to women. It would have required that sexual assault survivors be told about emergency contraception so they could avoid pregnancy. It would have required that the sex education taught in schools include information about contraception. It would have prevented health insurance companies from discriminating against women by refusing to pay for birth control.

I bet you never heard about this bill. Why? Because the anti-choice leadership in Congress never gave it a hearing and it certainly wasn't a priority for President [George W.] Bush. They were too busy passing vague, unconstitutional bans on abortions and doubling funding for ineffective abstinence-only-until-marriage sex education. That's what their "culture of life" looks like.

An Abortion Provider Is Murdered

Lou Michel and Dan Herbeck

James C. Kopp, an antiabortion activist, shot and killed abortion provider Barnett Slepian in 1998. In the following selection Lou Michel and Dan Herbeck recount their jailhouse interview with Kopp, during which he confesses to the crime. Kopp reveals that he did not intend to kill Slepian but only to prevent him from performing more abortions. He hopes that the jury will agree with his defense that he only meant to save unborn children. Kopp was convicted of second-degree murder in 2003 and was sentenced to twenty-five years to life in prison. Lou Michel and Dan Herbeck are journalists and are also coauthors of American Terrorist: Timothy McVeigh and the Oklahoma City Bombing.

James C. Kopp has admitted he shot and killed Dr. Barnett A. Slepian.

Kopp confessed to *The Buffalo News* that he planned the sniper shooting for a year, hid in the woods behind Slepian's Amherst [New York] home and fired the shot that killed the abortion provider.

In a jailhouse interview, Kopp said he scouted Slepian's neighborhood several times and also considered shooting other local doctors who provided abortions before he killed Slepian on Oct. 23, 1998.

Yet, despite that admission, Kopp maintains he is innocent of any crime.

Kopp said his outrage over abortion prompted him to shoot Slepian. He insists, however, that he intended to wound Slepian to prevent the physician from performing more abortions.

Lou Michel and Dan Herbeck, "Kopp Confesses; Tells News in Jail Interview. The Outrage About Abortion Prompted Shooting of Doctor," *Buffalo News*, November 20, 2002, p. A1. Copyright © 2002 by the *Buffalo News*. Reproduced by permission.

And he said he hopes that jurors will believe his account and understand his motives when his murder case goes to trial next year in Erie County Court.[1]

"The truth is not that I regret shooting Dr. Slepian. I regret that he died," Kopp said. "I aimed at his shoulder. The bullet took a crazy ricochet, and that's what killed him. One of my goals was to keep Dr. Slepian alive, and I failed at that goal."

Federal and local prosecutors do not accept Kopp's contention that he committed no crime.

"It doesn't change what we're going to do," District Attorney Frank J. Clark said. . . . "It just means there probably are fewer facts at issue."

Clark recently compared Slepian's killing to the [2002] wave of sniper killings in Washington, D.C.

"I consider this a crime of the worst magnitude," Clark said recently of the murder charge Kopp faces. "A man was gunned down in his own home, while his family was there. It was an assassination. To me, it's every bit as serious a crime as what is happening down in Washington."

Haunted by Feelings of Sorrow

Talking to two reporters in the Erie County Holding Center last week [November 2002], the 47-year-old abortion foe detailed the shooting and discussed his personal crusade against abortion that has taken him all over the world in the last two decades. His admissions are likely to surprise his supporters, especially those who say that he is a pacifist and a poor marksman, and that he was framed by the FBI.

Kopp said he decided to make a public confession because he feels badly that his supporters have been misled, and he wants them to know the truth about his actions and the reasons behind them. He said his only regret about the Amherst

1. Kopp was convicted of second-degree murder in 2003 and was sentenced to twenty-five years to life in prison.

shooting is that Slepian died. He said he is haunted by feelings of sorrow for Slepian's wife and four sons.

"To pick up a gun and aim it at another human being, and to fire, it's not a human thing to do," Kopp said in his opening statement of the interview. "It's not nice. It's not pleasant. It's gory, it's bloody. It overcomes every human instinct.

"The only thing that would be worse, to me, would be to do nothing, and to allow abortions to continue."

Among Kopp's other admissions during an interview that lasted more than four hours:

He selected Slepian's name out of a telephone book that listed abortion providers. Kopp said he had never read any news accounts about Slepian and had never participated in any Buffalo protests before the shooting. He said no one in the Buffalo pro-life community recommended Slepian as a target.

He checked out the homes of about six other Buffalo-area abortion providers before deciding that Slepian would be his target. He said his decision to target Slepian was based largely on the fact that Slepian's home was "vulnerable" because it had a rear window facing some woods.

Kopp said he scouted Slepian's neighborhood about six times, over the course of a year, before the attack. On two of those occasions, Kopp said, he had his gun and was ready to shoot if he saw Slepian at the rear window.

He insisted that he "tried very hard" to only wound Slepian. Kopp said he shot the physician in the back of his left shoulder and was "horrified" when he later learned that the bullet glanced off a bone and caused internal injuries that killed the doctor.

He declined to say whether he was involved in four similar, but nonfatal, shootings of abortion doctors in Perinton, Monroe County; Ancaster, Ont.; Vancouver, British Columbia; and Winnipeg, Manitoba.

Although he said he "acted alone" in the Slepian shooting, Kopp refused to say whether he ever received assistance from any person or organization. He also declined to explain why he buried his gun and other evidence in the woods behind the Slepian home.

Pro-Life Stance as Defense

Kopp's critics in the pro-choice community have accused him of being a cold-hearted assassin who used violence against those exercising their legal right to abortion.

In the years since the Slepian slaying, Kopp has been reviled as a vicious radical who used murder to destroy a family and further his anti-abortion agenda.

The killing of Slepian, in his own home, while his wife and four sons were nearby, shocked the community. Slepian, 52, also delivered babies and performed numerous other medical services for women. An abortion provider for 13 years, he had been applauded by members of the pro-choice community for his courage after facing numerous threats and protests.

Kopp said he understands why some people will accuse him of being a hypocrite advocating pro-life positions but shooting to death another human.

He said his attack on Slepian was consistent with his pro-life viewpoint, because it prevented Slepian from performing more abortions.

"I didn't intend to kill Dr. Slepian," Kopp said. "Why do you think I used force against Dr. Slepian when he was within 10 hours of taking the lives of 25 babies? The question answers itself."

Kopp's admission and his pro-life views are expected to be the basis of his defense, when his murder trial begins. That is scheduled for February [2003] in Erie County Court.

Kopp said he recently decided to change lawyers and go public with his confession because he had grown uncomfortable with a defense strategy that would have tried to convince jurors that he never shot Slepian.

Kopp insisted that "any idiot" who studies the Slepian case could see that the shooting was not intended to be fatal.

"I used force to restrain Dr. Slepian," he said. "I made every effort possible to make sure Dr. Slepian would not die. It's the easiest thing in the world to kill somebody with a rifle. You aim at the head or upper body. It's very, very difficult to just injure them, if that is your goal."

The Shooting Was Carefully Planned

A short, wiry man with a pale complexion, straight, reddish-brown hair and wire-rimmed glasses, Kopp kept a calm demeanor during most of the interview. At times, he became emotional as he discussed his anger over abortion, which he referred to as "the killing of babies, the killing of children." He described abortion clinics as "abortion mills."

Sitting beside him during the interview was his new attorney, Bruce A. Barket of Long Island. Barket encouraged Kopp to answer most of the questions posed to him, but occasionally jumped in to caution Kopp, telling him at one point that he should not discuss the shootings of other doctors.

"We'll defend one shooting at a time," Barket said.

Kopp, who used New York City as his base while traveling extensively to protest abortions in the last two decades, declined to say what prompted him to target a doctor in Western New York.

But in chilling detail, he explained how he selected Slepian as his victim, scouted the doctor's neighborhood and leaned against a tree about 90 feet behind the home on the night of Oct. 23, 1998, waiting to shoot the physician.

"I saw my target perfectly—crystal clear," Kopp said. "I saw him put the soup in the microwave and set the timer. Then, he moved away. I said to myself, 'He'll be returning to that exact spot in maybe 30 or 45 seconds.'"

Kopp said he squinted into the sight of his Soviet-made military rifle and aimed directly at the spot where Slepian's left rear shoulder would be positioned when he returned to the microwave.

"I aimed at his shoulder," said Kopp, who described himself as an expert shot. "I saw what I was aiming at. Only then did I fire."

Kopp said he was saddened the next night, when he found out the shot had killed Slepian.

"I did it, and I'm admitting it," he said. "But I never, ever intended for Dr. Slepian to die."

But Kopp also warned that other abortion foes might follow his lead and target people—particularly physicians involved in providing abortions.

"They're still in danger, absolutely," Kopp said. "I'm not the first, and I probably won't be the last." . . .

Never Meant to Kill

Several times during the interview, Kopp expressed regret that he killed Slepian. He said he thinks often about the Slepian family, and has a difficult time when he sees the doctor's widow, Lynne Slepian, sitting in court to watch his case.

"Whenever I see anyone who loved (Slepian), I feel very sad," Kopp said. "The thought of that happening to me, or people I care for, is absolutely terrible. To be sitting in a room, talking to your wife one minute, and in the next moment, to be shot, is terrifying."

But Kopp said he also believes that he saved the lives of some children by stopping Slepian from performing abortions.

"I strongly believe that," he said. "One misconception that people have is that I am a peaceful man who would not harm anybody. That is true, but at the same time, I am interested in saving and protecting babies.

"You don't go Jekyll-and-Hyde. You don't go crazy. To be peaceful is consistent with wanting to save children." ...

Even after admitting that he killed Slepian, Kopp believes there is a possibility that jurors will acquit him on all charges. He hopes jurors who hear his defense will conclude that he never meant to kill and that his sole intention was to protect unborn children.

Prosecutor Clark's recent comparison of Slepian's killing to the wave of sniper slayings in the Washington, D.C., area visibly angered Kopp.

"Any reasonable person could see a distinction between me and the D.C. sniper," Kopp said. "Why was Dr. Slepian shot? The obvious answer is to save children.

"If you did the same thing to protect a baby that was one day old, it would never be considered a crime."

Kopp was asked what he would do if he were acquitted and returned to the streets a free man. Would he shoot other doctors?

Kopp paused, and then answered the question.

"I would do something," he said.

He would not elaborate.

CHAPTER 4

Should Abortion Rights Be Restricted?

Chapter Preface

The abortion controversy is far more complex than deciding whether abortion should or should not be allowed. The issue is black and white only for those on the extreme ends of the debate: pro-life advocates who believe that abortion should never be allowed under any circumstances, and pro-choice advocates who hold that abortion on demand should be an unassailable right. For many others, the abortion issue is more complicated. Many pro-life supporters concede that there are some instances in which abortion should be permitted. And many pro-choice activists agree that some restrictions on abortion might be warranted.

A particularly thorny issue related to abortion is embryonic stem cell research. Many pro-life activists have retreated from the position that destroying an embryo for stem cell research amounts to abortion. President George W. Bush's bill severely limiting federal funding for embryonic stem cell research lost much of its support in Congress because many representatives had personal experience with the diseases that scientists say might be cured by stem cell research. These representatives argued that the greater good of helping sick people outweighs the protection of embryos.

Partial-birth abortion is another procedure that has been legislatively restricted. During a partial-birth abortion, which is performed late in a pregnancy, a doctor partially delivers the fetus and then punctures the back of the skull and removes the brain before completing delivery. The procedure is often elected when doctors discover that the fetus has severe abnormalities. President Bush has tried to establish a ban on partial-birth abortion, but several lower courts have overturned it. In the meantime, many pro-choice advocates have remained quiet on the issue because of their discomfort with the nature of the procedure.

Other efforts to restrict abortion include attempts to enact parental notification and consent laws so that minors cannot obtain an abortion unless their parents have been informed or agree to the procedure. Also, some state legislatures are considering conscience clause bills. These laws would allow medical professionals who are morally opposed to birth control and abortion to refuse to provide these services. The laws would also extend to pharmacists, allowing them to refuse to fill prescriptions for birth control and emergency contraception. People on both sides of the abortion debate continue to wrangle over these restrictions.

Since the 1992 U.S. Supreme Court ruling in *Planned Parenthood v. Casey*, which gave individual state governments the ability to pass their own laws regulating abortion, pro-life activists have increased their efforts to legislatively restrict abortion. On the pro-choice side, activists work to fight these restrictions and expand access to reproductive health services. Now that the Supreme Court has two new members, both of whom are considered conservative, many commentators believe that further restrictions on abortion procedures seem likely. In consequence, the debate over this most complex of issues is sure to continue.

The Partial Birth Abortion Ban Defends Innocent Children

George W. Bush

Partial birth abortion is a late-term procedure in which the fetus is delivered before being killed. In 2003 Congress passed the Partial Birth Abortion Ban Act, which prohibited the procedure. The following is an excerpt from President George W. Bush's remarks from November 5, 2003, the day he signed the bill into law. In his comments Bush praises Congress for passing legislation that defends innocent children and outlawing a procedure that violates medical ethics. The new law was challenged almost immediately in three federal courts, where it was overturned. The Bush administration has appealed the case to the Supreme Court, where a decision was pending as this volume went to press.

Good afternoon. I'm pleased that all of you have joined us as the Partial Birth Abortion Ban Act of 2003 becomes the law of the land. For years, a terrible form of violence has been directed against children who are inches from birth, while the law looked the other way.... At last, the American people and our government have confronted the violence and come to the defense of the innocent child....

In passing this legislation, members of the House and Senate made a studied decision based upon compelling evidence. The best case against partial birth abortion is a simple description of what happens and to whom it happens. It involves the partial delivery of a live boy or girl, and a sudden, violent end of that life. Our nation owes its children a different and better welcome. The bill I am about to sign protecting innocent new life from this practice reflects the compassion and humanity of America.

George W. Bush, "President Bush Signs Partial Birth Abortion Ban Act of 2003," www-.whitehouse.gov, November 5, 2003.

The Bill Affirms a Basic Standard of Humanity

In the course of the congressional debate, the facts became clear. Each year, thousands of partial birth abortions are committed. As Doctor C. Everett Koop, the pediatrician and former Surgeon General has pointed out, the majority of partial birth abortions are not required by medical emergency. As Congress has found, the practice is widely regarded within the medical profession as unnecessary, not only cruel to the child, but harmful to the mother, and a violation of medical ethics.

The facts about partial birth abortion are troubling and tragic, and no lawyer's brief can make them seem otherwise. By acting to prevent this practice, the elected branches of our government have affirmed a basic standard of humanity, the duty of the strong to protect the weak. The wide agreement amongst men and women on this issue, regardless of political party, shows that bitterness in political debate can be overcome by compassion and the power of conscience. And the executive branch will vigorously defend this law against any who would try to overturn it in the courts.

America stands for liberty, for the pursuit of happiness and for the unalienable right of life. And the most basic duty of government is to defend the life of the innocent. Every person, however frail or vulnerable, has a place and a purpose in this world. Every person has a special dignity. This right to life cannot be granted or denied by government, because it does not come from government, it comes from the Creator of life.

In the debate about the rights of the unborn, we are asked to broaden the circle of our moral concern. We're asked to live out our calling as Americans. We're asked to honor our own standards, announced on the day of our founding in the Declaration of Independence. We're asked by our convictions and tradition and compassion to build a culture of life, and make this a more just and welcoming society. And today, we welcome vulnerable children into the care and protection of Americans.

The late Pennsylvania Governor Robert Casey once said that: when we look to the unborn child, the real issue is not when life begins, but when love begins. This is the generous and merciful spirit of our country at its best. This spirit is reflected in the Partial Birth Abortion Ban Act of 2003, which I am now honored to sign into law. God bless.

Thank you, all.

The Partial Birth Abortion Ban Should Be Repealed

Kim Gandy

When President George W. Bush signed into law the 2003 Partial Birth Abortion Ban Act—which prohibited a procedure in which a fetus is delivered before being killed—abortion-rights groups reacted strongly. The following statement is a response to the new law from the National Organization for Women [NOW]. In it, NOW president Kim Gandy argues that the term "partial birth abortion" is not a valid medical term but rather a fabrication by pro-life groups. Gandy vows that women's rights activists will work to keep abortion safe, legal and accessible. The law was overturned, and the case is now being appealed. Gandy has served NOW at the local, state, and national level since 1973 and has been president since 2001.

Today [Nov. 2003, President] George W. Bush sends a message to every woman and girl in the United States—your reproductive rights are not guaranteed. By signing the deceptively-named Partial-Birth Abortion Ban into law, Bush confirms that his administration and Congress have both the power and the will to overturn *Roe v. Wade* [which legalized abortion], one step at a time. This is the first ban on an abortion procedure since abortion became legal in 1973, but it will not be the last if George W. Bush remains in office.

NOW [National Organization for Women] activists are here today to bear witness to this travesty—the theft of our reproductive freedom and our constitutional rights, and this administration's complete disregard for the welfare of women across this country. The so-called Partial-Birth Abortion Ban

Statement of NOW President Kim Gandy, "Bush Takes Away Women's Reproductive Rights—Feminists Promise to Vote Him Out of Office," www.now.org, November 5, 2003. Copyright © 2003 by the National Organization for Women. Reproduced by permission.

is a dangerous piece of legislation that ultimately seeks to out-law even the safest abortion procedures. The truth is that the term 'partial birth abortion' doesn't exist in the medical world—it's a fabrication of the anti-choice machine. The law doesn't even contain an exception to preserve a woman's health and future fertility, and it will have a chilling effect on the ability of physicians to offer women the best, most appropriate medical care at all times.

The Law Should Be Invalidated

The federal courts and, ultimately, the Supreme Court, may be our only recourse to invalidate this regressive law. Our courts are not yet controlled by conservative extremists, but that is Bush's goal. Right now, the Supreme Court narrowly supports a woman's right to make her own reproductive decisions. By the time the challenge to this law reaches the Supreme Court, we could have one or two new justices who do not believe in a woman's constitutional right to abortion. Once that final piece of the puzzle is in place—and the right-wing controls all three branches of government—*Roe v. Wade* will only be a memory.

Women's rights activists across the country are recommitting ourselves to keeping abortion safe, legal and accessible. We will not allow Bush and his buddies to erode our rights. We will take our case to the courts, to the streets and to the ballot box. We will restore women's right to privacy and their access to critical medical procedures; we will march on Washington next year on April 25 to Save Women's Lives; and we will remember in November [2004].

Parental Notification Law Will Protect Minors

William P. Clark, Mary L. Davenport, and Maria Guadalupe Garcia

Most states have adopted laws that require parents to be notified when minors seek an abortion, and some even require that parents consent to the procedure. The following viewpoint argues in favor of a proposed constitutional amendment that would require parental notification for a minor seeking an abortion in California. William P. Clark, Mary L. Davenport, and Maria Guadalupe Garcia contend that the law would allow parents to help their daughters with the physical and emotional consequences resulting from abortion. They further argue that it would have a deterrent effect, reducing pregnancies and abortions among minors. The initiative was narrowly defeated in the November 2005 election. Clark is a retired California Supreme Court justice, and Davenport is a physician and a fellow of the American College of Obstetricians and Gynecologists. Garcia is the organizing director of Parents' Right to Know and Child Protection/Yes on 73.

In California, a daughter under 18 can't get an aspirin from the school nurse, get a flu shot, or have a tooth pulled without a parent knowing.

However, surgical or chemical abortions can be secretly performed on minor girls—even *13 years old or younger—without parents' knowledge.*

Parents are then not prepared to help young daughters with any of the serious physical, emotional, or psychological complications which may result from an abortion or to protect their daughters from further sexual exploitation and pregnancies.

William P. Clark, Mary L. Davenport, and Maria Guadalupe Garcia, "Argument in Favor of Proposition 73," *California Official Voter Information Guide,* August 2005.

A study of over 46,000 pregnancies of school-age girls in California found that *over two-thirds* were impregnated by adult men whose mean age was 22.6 years.

Investigations have shown that secret abortions on minors in California are rarely reported to child protective services although these pregnancies are evidence of statutory rape and sexual abuse. This leaves these girls *vulnerable* to further sexual abuse, rapes, pregnancies, abortions, and sexually transmitted diseases.

That's *why more than one million signatures* were submitted to allow Californians to *vote* on the "Parents' Right to Know and Child Protection" Proposition 73.[1]

Prop. 73 will require that one parent or guardian be notified at least 48 hours before an abortion is performed on a minor daughter.

Most People Support Parental Notification Laws

Parents and daughters in more than 30 other states have benefited for years from laws like Prop. 73. Many times, after such laws pass, there have been substantial reductions in pregnancies and abortions among minors.

When parents are involved and minors cannot anticipate secret access to free abortions they more often avoid the reckless behavior which leads to pregnancies. Older men, including Internet predators, are deterred from impregnating minors when secret abortions are not available to conceal their crimes.

If she chooses, a minor may petition juvenile court to permit an abortion without notifying a parent. She can request a lawyer to help her. If the evidence shows she is mature enough to decide for herself or that notifying a parent is not in her best interests, the judge will grant her petition. The proceedings must be confidential, prompt, and free. She may also seek

1. The proposition did not pass.

help from juvenile court if she is being coerced by anyone to consent to an abortion.

Polls show most people support parental notification laws. They know that a minor girl—pregnant, scared, and possibly abandoned or pressured by an older boyfriend—needs the advice and support of a *parent*.

Parents have invested more attention and love in raising their daughter, know her personal and medical history better, and care more about her future than strangers employed by abortion clinics profiting from performing many abortions on minors.

A minor still has a right to obtain or refuse an abortion, but a parent can help her understand all options, obtain competent care, and provide medical records and history.

An informed parent can also get prompt care for *hemorrhage, infections*, and other possibly *fatal* complications.

Vote "YES" on Prop. 73 to allow parents to care for and protect their minor daughters!

Parental Notification Law Will Endanger Teenagers

Robert L. Black, Ruth E. Haskins, and Deborah Burger

In 2005 a proposition appeared on the California ballot that would require parents to be notified when minors seek an abortion. The following viewpoint argues against the proposed constitutional amendment. Robert L. Black, Ruth E. Haskins, and Deborah Burger assert that family communication should begin before a teen faces an unplanned pregnancy. They argue that the law would place a terrifying burden on girls who do not feel safe discussing their pregnancy with their parents. The initiative was narrowly defeated in the November 2005 election. Black is a physician and an officer of the board of the American Academy of Pediatrics. Haskins is chairperson of the Committee on Legislation for the American College of Obstetricians and Gynecologists. Burger is president of the California Nurses Association.

Parents rightfully want to be involved in their teenagers' lives and all parents want what is best for their children. But good family communication can't be imposed by government.

Parents care most about keeping their children safe. That means always safe, even if they feel they can't come to us and tell us everything.

Family communication must begin long before a teen faces an unplanned pregnancy. *The best way to protect our daughters is to begin talking about responsible, appropriate sexual behavior from the time they are young and fostering an atmosphere that assures them they can come to us.*

Even teenagers who have good relationships with their parents might be afraid to talk to them about something as sensitive as pregnancy.

Robert L. Black, Ruth E. Haskins, and Deborah Burger, "Argument Against Proposition 73," *California Official Voter Information Guide*, August 2005.

And sadly, some teens live in troubled homes. The family might be having serious problems, or parents might be abusive, or a relative may even have caused the pregnancy.

This law [proposition 73] puts those vulnerable teenagers—those who most need protection—in harm's way, or forces them to go to court.[1] Think about it: the girl is already terrified, she's pregnant, her family is abusive or worse. She's not going to be marching up to a judge in a crowded courthouse. *She doesn't need a judge, she needs a counselor.*

Law Would Endanger Teenagers

Mandatory notification laws make scared, pregnant teens who can't go to their parents do scary things, instead of going to the doctor to get the medical help they need. In other states, when parental notification laws make teenagers choose between talking with parents or having illegal or unsafe abortions, some teens choose the illegal abortion—even though it is dangerous. Sometimes teenagers are just teenagers.

And if, in desperation, teenagers turn to illegal, self-induced or back-alley abortions many will suffer serious injuries and some will die.

The California Nurses Association, California Academy of Family Physicians, and the California Medical Association all oppose proposition 73. Mandatory notification laws may sound good, but, in the real world, they just put teenagers in real danger.

The real answer to teen pregnancy is prevention, and strong, caring families—not new laws that endanger our daughters.

California's teen pregnancy rate dropped significantly over the last decade without constitutional amendments or forced notification laws. That's because doctors, nurses, parents, teachers, and counselors are teaching teenagers about responsibility, abstinence, and birth control. These programs will help keep our daughters safe and out of trouble.

1. The proposition did not pass.

Talking to our daughters when they are young and fostering a place where they can freely communicate is the best solution.

But if—*for whatever reason*—our daughters can't or they won't come to us, we must make sure they get safe, professional medical attention and quality counseling from caring doctors and nurses.

As parents, we want to know when our daughters face a decision like this so we can be helpful and supportive. But also, as parents, our daughters' safety is more important than our desire to be informed.

Please join us in voting NO on Proposition 73.

Embryonic Stem Cell Research Destroys Human Life

William H. Keeler

Many scientists laud embryonic stem cell research as the most promising line of research into a cure for cancer and other diseases. However, many abortion foes object to the research, contending that it is tantamount to abortion because an embryo is destroyed when stem cells are harvested from it. In 2001 President George W. Bush signed legislation that limited federal funds for embryonic stem cell research to stem cell lines already in existence. In 2005 legislation was proposed to ease the restrictions. In the following selection William H. Keeler writes to the U.S. Senate to express the Catholic Church's opposition to the House of Representatives bill HR 810 and its companion bill in the Senate, S 471, which would expand the number of embryos available for research. Keeler contends that the government should not force taxpayers to participate in destroying human life. He also argues that the promise of stem cell research has been exaggerated. The House bill passed in May 2005, and as this volume went to press, it was pending in the Senate. Keeler is the archbishop of Baltimore and the chairman of the Committee for Pro-Life Activities of the U.S. Conference of Catholic Bishops.

The Senate may soon vote on whether federal funds should be used to encourage large-scale destruction of innocent human life for research purposes.[1] H.R. 810/S. 471, the Specter/Harkin bill on stem cell research, would rescind President [George W.] Bush's policy on embryonic stem cell (ESC) research, so the offer of federal funds for such research can be

1. The bill passed the House but was pending in the Senate as this volume went to press.

William H. Keeler, letter to the U.S. Senate, www.usccb.org, July 11, 2005.

used to encourage researchers to destroy new human embryos from fertility clinics for their cells. I urge you in the strongest possible terms to oppose all destructive and morally offensive proposals of this kind.

Government has no business forcing taxpayers to become complicit in the direct destruction of human life at any stage. Nor is there any point in denying the scientific fact that human life is exactly what is at stake here.

Even government advisory groups recommending destructive embryo research have recognized that human embryos "deserve respect as a form of human life" [according to the National Bioethics Advisory Commission, 1999]. What these groups have never managed to show is how one can claim to "respect" human beings one is treating as mere crops for harvesting.

Rightly rejecting such a crass utilitarian approach, since 1995 Congress has passed—and Presidents of both major parties have signed—annual riders insisting that early human embryos be protected from risk of harm or death in federally funded research projects. H.R. 810 radically departs from this precedent by encouraging researchers to kill human embryos, or pay others to kill them, to become eligible for federal stem cell research grants.

An Immoral Decision

The argument that these human embryos "would be discarded anyway" carries no moral weight. The fact that many abortions are performed in the U.S. creates no argument that Congress must use its funding power to promote such killing. By the same token, the fact that condemned prisoners or terminally ill patients will "die soon anyway" gives no government, and indeed no individual, a special right to conduct lethal experiments on them. In the case of human embryos now frozen in fertility clinics, this argument also rests on a false factual premise, because embryos already selected by their parents for discarding are barred from being used in research and vice versa. On the other hand, if Congress is trying to influence *future* decisions by parents tempted to discard embryos, why would it intervene to encourage destruction for research, instead of encouraging a decision to let their embryonic children survive? The obvious answer is that Congress will have made its own immoral decision that these developing human beings are worth more dead than alive.

It would be bad enough to promote such destruction of life if it had been found necessary to save patients with devastating diseases. In such a case it would be important to remember that the end, however worthwhile in itself, does not justify an evil means. But in fact, the practical argument for funding ESC research fails even on its own amoral terms. For adult stem cells and other avenues posing no moral problem have advanced quickly toward human clinical trials to treat juvenile diabetes, corneal damage, Parkinson's disease, spinal cord injury, sickle-cell anemia, cardiac damage and many other conditions. (For details see www.stemcellresearch.org.) At the same time, researchers increasingly acknowledge that the apparent initial "promise" of ESCs was exaggerated. For example, because of their genetic instability and tendency to form potentially lethal tumors in host animals, these cells may not be ready for human clinical trials for many years, if ever. (See www.usccb.org/prolife/issues/bioethic/stemcell/obstacles51004.htm.)

At this point in medical science, the question is not whether alternative ways are available to pursue the therapeutic goals served by ESCs—rather, it is whether ESCs will ever catch up with the therapeutic benefits now arising from the alternatives. After decades of research in animal ESCs and over six years of concentrated research on human ESCs, no safe and effective therapeutic use for ESCs has been discovered. Even the utilitarian argument for forcing taxpayers to fund ESC research lacks any firm basis in the facts.

The current federal policy of funding research on a limited number of existing ESC lines has achieved its stated goal—that of exploring which avenues of stem cell research will most quickly and effectively lead to promising treatments. The emerging answer is that ESC research is not one of those avenues. If there is to be any change in the existing policy, it should be to end this limited funding of ESC research altogether, so taxpayers' resources can more effectively be marshaled for research now showing itself to be more ethically *and* medically sound.

To insist now on a *broader* policy of promoting ESC research, using federal funds to encourage more destruction of human embryos, would fly in the face of the medical evidence and violate even the most minimal standards of respect for early human life. I urge you to reject H.R. 810/S. 471 and any similar proposal, and instead to support promising medical research that all Americans can live with.

Embryonic Stem Cell Research Is Moral

William Frist

Republican senator William (Bill) Frist, a physician, believes that embryonic stem cells can be used to find a cure for cancer and other diseases. Because of this belief he supports Senate bill S 471, which would increase the number of stem cell lines that could be used for research. In the following excerpt from his remarks delivered to the Senate on July 29, 2005, Frist explores the moral and ethical challenges associated with embryonic stem cell research. He concludes that using embryos for stem cell research that are destined to be discarded does not violate moral or ethical principles, and he argues federal funding for the research should be expanded. The companion bill in the House of Representatives, HR 810, passed in May 2005. As this volume went to press, S 471 was pending in the Senate. Frist is a senator from Tennessee and is the Senate majority leader.

Since 2001 when stem cell research first captured our nation's attention, I've said many times the issue will have to be reviewed on an ongoing basis—and not just because the science holds tremendous promise, or because it's developing with breathtaking speed. Indeed, stem cell research presents the first major moral and ethical challenge to biomedical research in the 21st century. . . .

If we can answer the moral and ethical questions about stem cell research, I believe we will have the opportunity to save many lives and make countless other lives more fulfilling. That's why we must get our stem cell policy right—scientifically and ethically. And that's why I stand on the floor of the United States Senate today [July 29, 2005].

Four years ago, I came to this floor and laid out a comprehensive proposal to promote stem cell research within a thor-

William Frist, statement before the U.S. Senate, Washington, DC, January 29, 2005.

ough framework of ethics. I proposed 10 specific interdependent principles. They dealt with all types of stem cell research, including adult and embryonic stem cells.

As we know, adult stem cell research is not controversial on ethical grounds—while embryonic stem cell research is. Right now, to derive embryonic stem cells, an embryo—which many, including myself, consider nascent human life—must be destroyed. But I also strongly believe—as do countless other scientists, clinicians, and doctors—that embryonic stem cells uniquely hold specific promise for some therapies and potential cures that adult stem cells cannot provide.

I'll come back to that later. Right now, though, let me say this: I believe today—as I believed and stated in 2001, prior to the establishment of current policy—that the federal government should fund embryonic stem cell research. And as I said four years ago, we should federally fund research only on embryonic stem cells derived from blastocysts left over from fertility therapy, which will not be implanted or adopted but instead are otherwise destined by the parents with absolute certainty to be discarded and destroyed.

Ethical Oversight

Let me read to you my 5th principle as I presented it on this floor four years ago:

No. 5. Provide funding for embryonic stem cell research only from blastocysts that would otherwise be discarded. We need to allow Federal funding for research using only those embryonic stem cells derived from blastocysts that are left over after in vitro fertilization and would otherwise be discarded.

I made it clear at the time, and do so again today, that such funding should only be provided within a system of comprehensive ethical oversight. Federally funded embryonic research should be allowed only with transparent and fully informed consent of the parents. And that consent should be granted under a careful and thorough federal regulatory system, which considers both science and ethics. Such a comprehensive ethical system, I believe, is absolutely essential. Only with strict safeguards, public accountability, and complete transparency will we ensure that this new, evolving research unfolds within accepted ethical bounds.

My comprehensive set of 10 principles, as outlined in 2001 are as follows:

1. Ban Embryo Creation for Research;

2. Continue Funding Ban on Derivation;

3. Ban Human Cloning;

4. Increase Adult Stem Cell Research Funding;

5. Provide Funding for Embryonic Stem Cell Research Only From Blastocysts That Would Otherwise Be Discarded;

6. Require a Rigorous Informed Consent Process;

7. Limit Number of Stem Cell Lines;

8. Establish A Strong Public Research Oversight System;

9. Require Ongoing, Independent Scientific and Ethical Review;

10. Strengthen and Harmonize Fetal Tissue Research Restrictions.

That is what I said four years ago, and that is what I believe today. After all, principles are meant to stand the test of time—even when applied to a field changing as rapidly as stem cell research.

Great Promise to Heal

I'm a physician. My profession is healing. I've devoted my life to attending to the needs of the sick and suffering and to promoting health and well being. For the past several years, I've temporarily set aside the profession of medicine to participate in public policy with a continued commitment to heal.

In all forms of stem cell research, I see today, just as I saw in 2001, great promise to heal. Whether it's diabetes, Parkinson's disease, heart disease, Lou Gehrig's disease, or spinal cord injuries, stem cells offer hope for treatment that other lines of research cannot offer.

Embryonic stem cells have specific properties that make them uniquely powerful and deserving of special attention in the realm of medical science. These special properties explain why scientists and physicians feel so strongly about support of embryonic as well as adult stem cell research.

Unlike other stem cells, embryonic stem cells are "pluripotent." That means they have the capacity to become any type of tissue in the human body. Moreover, they are capable of renewing themselves and replicating themselves over and over again—indefinitely.

Adult stem cells meet certain medical needs. But embryonic stem cells—because of these unique characteristics—meet other medical needs that simply cannot be met today by adult stem cells. They especially offer hope for treating a range of diseases that require tissue to regenerate or restore function.

President's Policy Should Be Modified

On August 9, 2001, shortly after I outlined my principles, President [George W.] Bush announced his policy on embryonic stem cell research. His policy was fully consistent with my ten principles, so I strongly supported it. It federally funded embryonic stem cell research for the first time. It did so within an ethical framework. And it showed respect for human life.

But this policy restricted embryonic stem cell funding only to those cell lines that had been derived from embryos before the date of his announcement. In my policy I, too, proposed restricting number of cell lines, but I did not propose a specific cutoff date. Over time, with a limited number of cell lines, would we be able to realize the full promise of embryonic stem cell research?

When the President announced his policy, it was widely believed that 78 embryonic stem cell lines would be available for federal funding. That has proven not to be the case. Today only 22 lines are eligible. Moreover, those lines unexpectedly after several generations are starting to become less stable and less replicative than initially thought (they are acquiring and losing chromosomes, losing the normal karyotype,[1] and potentially losing growth control). They also were grown on mouse feeder cells, which we have learned since, will likely limit their future potential for clinical therapy in humans (e.g., potential of viral contamination).

While human embryonic stem cell research is still at a very early stage, the limitations put in place in 2001 will, over time, slow our ability to bring potential new treatments for certain diseases. Therefore, I believe the President's policy should be modified. We should expand federal funding (and thus NIH [National Institutes of Health] oversight) and current guidelines governing stem cell research, carefully and thoughtfully staying within ethical bounds.

---

1. the chromosomal makeup of a cell, arranged in order from largest to smallest

Health Care Workers Should Be Allowed to Refuse to Participate in Abortion

Mary A. Klaver

*Conscience clause legislation, which would give health care work-
ers the right to refuse to participate in certain services such as
abortion, has been working its way through state legislatures.
The following selection is Mary A. Klaver's testimony before the
Wisconsin State Assembly Labor Committee in support of a 2003
proposed bill that would affirm and extend Wisconsin's existing
protections. Klaver states that the new law is clearer in protecting
medical professionals who decline to provide abortion services.
She also offers her support for other components of the bill. One
such component establishes protection for pharmacists who refuse
to fill prescriptions for birth control and morning-after pills,
which are taken after sexual intercourse and prevent ovulation,
fertilization, or implantation. Although the bill passed in the
Wisconsin legislature, Governor Jim Doyle vetoed it in 2004.
Klaver is the legislative legal counsel for Wisconsin Right to Life.*

Representative [Stephen] Nass and members of the [Wis-
consin State Assembly Labor] committee, my name is
Mary Klaver. I am the Legislative Legal Counsel for Wisconsin
Right to Life. I appear today in support of Assembly Bill 67,
the conscience clause bill.[1]

In today's world, more and more health care providers
find that some health care practices raise serious moral concerns. Social, legal, and medical developments involving abor-

1. The bill was passed in the legislature but Wisconsin governor Jim Doyle vetoed it in
2004.

Mary A. Klaver, testimony before the Wisconsin State Assembly Labor Committee,
March 5, 2005.

tion, assisted suicide, euthanasia, withdrawal of feeding tubes, human embryo destruction, embryonic stem cell research and fetal tissue transplants have put health care providers in the center of some of society's most controversial moral dilemmas. As medical technology evolves, the ethical dilemmas for Wisconsin's health care providers will continue to grow.

Fortunately, the federal government and most states have enacted "conscience clauses"—statutes intended to protect the right of health care providers to refuse to provide or participate in certain procedures to which they have moral or religious objections. Unfortunately, nearly all of these statutes are severely limited in their application. Most conscience clause provisions were adopted between 1973 and 1982, when the courts were broadly defining a new and very controversial constitutional privacy right to abortion. Consequently, most conscience clause statutes only protect the right to refuse to participate in an abortion. Some states also protect the right to refuse to participate in sterilization, contraception or artificial insemination. One state (Wyoming) covers euthanasia. Only one state statute (Illinois) provides conscience rights protection for all medical procedures.

The Current Law Is Unclear

Wisconsin's current conscience clause statute, s. 253.09, has been on the books since 1973. Section 253.09: (1) protects the right of a hospital to refuse to admit any patient or to allow the use of the hospital facilities "for the purpose of performing a sterilization procedure or [an abortion]", (2) protects the right of a "physician or any other person who is a member of or associated with the staff of a hospital, or any employee of a hospital" to refuse to participate or assist in a sterilization procedure or an abortion, if the objection is in writing and based on moral or religious grounds, (3) protects "any person" from discrimination in employment, student status or staff status on the "ground that the person refuses to recommend, aid or perform procedures for sterilization or [abortion], if the refusal is based on religious or moral precepts", and (4) protects individuals and entities who receive "any grant, contract, loan or loan guarantee under any state or federal law" from being required to participate in various ways in a sterilization procedure or an abortion if this would be contrary to the religious beliefs or moral convictions of the individual, the entity or the personnel of the entity.

Also, under Wisconsin law, civil immunity is provided for hospitals and hospital employees (s. 253.09), physicians (s. 448.03 (5) (a)) and nurses (s. 441.06 (6)) for any civil damages resulting from a refusal to perform a sterilization procedure or an abortion, if such refusal is based on religious or moral precepts. It is unclear whether or not Wisconsin's conscience clause statute provides professional immunity in these circumstances. The provision in s. 253.09 (1) prohibiting "any disciplinary or recriminatory action" against a "physician or any other person who is a member of or associated with the staff of a hospital, or any employee of a hospital" who refuses to participate or assist in a sterilization procedure or an abortion may provide professional immunity, but this is not clear.

Proposed Law Extends Protections

Assembly Bill 67 extends the current protections under Wisconsin's conscience clause law by doing all of the following:

1. Extending the protection of Wisconsin's current conscience clause law to other related issues such as the use of abortifacients, destruction of or experimentation on human embryos, use of fetal tissues from aborted babies, withholding or withdrawal of nutrition or hydration, assisted suicide, and euthanasia.

2. Creating a conscience clause law for pharmacists who are not covered by the current law.

3. Clarifying that each of these conscience clause laws

grants protection from employment discrimination, professional liability and civil liability.

4. Granting persons whose conscience rights are being violated the right to sue for injunctive relief, damages and attorney fees.

Last session, there was some concern about adding conscience clause protections to the fair employment law under the existing provision prohibiting employment discrimination based upon "creed". This is actually nothing more than a clarification of existing law. As I noted earlier, s. 253.09 already has a prohibition on discrimination in employment, student status or staff status on the ground that "any person" refuses to recommend, aid or perform procedures for sterilization or abortion, if the refusal is based on religious or moral precepts. However, no one seems to know who has enforcement responsibility for this provision. Several years ago, Wisconsin Right to Life asked the Department of Health and Family Services for advice on the enforcement responsibility for s. 253.09. According to the Department Legal Counsel, no single agency is responsible for enforcement of this statute. It makes sense, then, to clarify that the Equal Rights Division has enforcement responsibility in the primary area of concern, which is employment discrimination against health care providers. Physicians, nurses, hospital employees, pharmacists and other health care providers deserve the full protection of Wisconsin's fair employment law to protect their right to refuse to participate in the wide range of activities protected by this legislation. The discrimination based on creed provision is an integral part of the conscience clause protection package.

In addition, Assembly Bill 67 allows a person who is adversely affected by conduct that violates the conscience clause provisions to bring a private civil action for injunctive relief, damages, and attorney's fees.

Wisconsin Right to Life urges this committee to vote in favor of Assembly Bill 67 and protect the right of the health care providers in this state to practice their professions in a life-affirming manner without jeopardizing their means of livelihood.

Health Care Workers Should Not Be Allowed to Refuse to Participate in Abortions

Sue Moline Larson

Wisconsin is one of many states considering conscience clause legislation, which would give health care workers the right to refuse to participate in certain services—including abortion, sterilization, and assisted suicide—if they are morally opposed to them. In the following selection Sue Moline Larson appeals to the Wisconsin State Assembly to vote against a 2003 bill that would expand Wisconsin's existing conscience clause protections. Larson cites the Lutheran Church's position on abortion, which counters the idea that personal preference is more important than providing services to those who seek medical assistance. She also argues that the bill's underlying purpose seems to be an attempt to limit reproductive choice. Although the bill passed in the Wisconsin legislature, Governor Jim Doyle vetoed it in 2004. Larson is the director of the Lutheran Office for Public Policy in Wisconsin.

The Wisconsin State Assembly is scheduled to vote this week [June 2003] on AB 67, "conscience clause" legislation.[1] The Lutheran Office for Public Policy in Wisconsin, the legislative voice of the six synods of the Evangelical Lutheran Church in America [ELCA] with 750 congregations in the state, opposes this bill. The ELCA affirms both a freedom and an obligation to engage in serious deliberation on moral issues such as those raised by AB 67. The bill would exempt medical professionals from participating in serving the public based on their personal beliefs. At its 1991 national church

---

1. The Bill was passed in the legislature but Wisconsin governor Jim Doyle vetoed it in 2004.

Sue Moline Larson, "Opposition to Conscience Clause Legislation," www.loppw.org, June 4, 2003.

wide assembly, the ELCA adopted a social teaching statement on abortion. That statement lifts up the concerns of caring for those who are most vulnerable, and effective service to the neighbor as mandates for people of faith.

The Abortion statement counters the premise that personal preferences supersede conscientious service by health care providers in the fields they have chosen to work. The church believes that professionally trained people are bound to act with competence and to respect the needs and integrity of those who seek medical assistance. Professional guidelines require an objectivity and willingness that honors the pledge to serve a greater good than that expressed by one's own perspectives and preferences.

The Bill Hinders Reproductive Choice

The purpose of law is to protect the general welfare of all in society. AB 67 promotes the preferences of some at the expense of the many. This church stands firmly behind the right of contraception to be available for those who wish to utilize it, and upholds the rights of individuals who seek voluntary sterilization to prevent unwanted pregnancies. This bill compromises the availability to both of those significant health needs. Because the state of Wisconsin does not permit assisted suicide, or euthanasia, two procedures that this bill would protect medical professionals from participating in, its underlying purpose seems primarily to be the further hindering of reproductive choice.

The ELCA Abortion statement warns against unduly encumbering or endangering the lives of women by proposing regulations that generate problems worse than any such regulations would seek to address. AB 67 falls into that category. The ELCA also strongly opposes legislation that is primarily intended to harass those who seek contraceptives or who contemplate termination of a pregnancy. By proposing to protect professionals, this bill will allow them to deny access to information, medication and safe treatment options. That is particularly egregious in light of the medical assistance needs of women and girls who have survived abuse or rape. Their well-being should always be a higher priority than the desires of those who may or may not wish to provide them treatment.

The social statement states, "One of the clearest ways in which a society both expresses its attitudes and values, and shapes them, is through law." To shape just public policy through law, justice must be sought for all. AB 67 does not establish just policy, rather, it has been designed to subvert it. For that reason, we urge you to vote against this bill.

Chronology

2600 B.C.

A recipe for an herbal drug to induce abortion is first recorded.

Fourth Century B.C.

The philosopher Aristotle argues that abortion is allowable until the human soul develops, approximately the fortieth day of gestation.

Fourth Century A.D.

St. Augustine expresses the mainstream view that early abortion requires penance only for sexual sin.

Thirteenth Century

St. Thomas Aquinas, relying on the philosophy and biology of Aristotle, writes that the soul is not infused into the body until forty days after conception. He teaches that after that point abortion is a grave evil.

1588

Pope Sixtus forbids all abortions.

1591

Pope Gregory XIV overturns Pope Sixtus's edict against abortion.

1821

Connecticut passes the first law in the United States prohibiting abortions after "quickening."

1869

Pope Pius IX forbids all abortions, a stance from which the Catholic Church has not since wavered.

1873

Congress passes the Comstock Law, which prohibits sending information and devices for the prevention of conception through the mail.

1916

Margaret Sanger opens the first birth control clinic in the United States.

1937

North Carolina becomes the first state to recognize birth control as a public health measure and provides contraceptive services to low-income mothers through its public health programs.

1942

The American Birth Control League changes its name to Planned Parenthood Federation of America and begins advocating abortion law reforms.

1950

Illegal abortions in the United States are estimated to be between 200,000 and 1.3 million.

1962

Denied an abortion in Phoenix, television star Sherri Finkbine goes to Stockholm to abort a fetus with severe birth defects caused by the drug thalidomide.

1965

In *Griswold v. Connecticut* the Supreme Court establishes the constitutional right to privacy, laying the groundwork for *Roe v. Wade*.

1966

The National Organization for Women is founded.

1967

Twenty-five state legislatures consider abortion reform bills.

1969

The first National Conference on Abortion Laws is held, during which the National Association for Repeal of Abortion Laws (NARAL) is founded.

1970

New York, Washington, and Hawaii become the first states to repeal criminal abortion laws.

1973

On January 22 the U.S. Supreme Court hands down its decision in *Roe v. Wade*, legalizing abortion.

1973

On May 14 the National Right to Life Committee is incorporated.

1973

Responding to anti–*Roe v. Wade* backlash, the reproductive rights organization NARAL changes its name to National Abortion Rights Action League.

1976

The Hyde Amendment limits Medicaid-funded abortions for poor women except in the case of medical emergency.

1976

The Supreme Court's *Planned Parenthood v. Danforth* decision says states cannot give husbands veto power over their wives' decision to abort their pregnancies. The Court also says parents of minor, unwed girls cannot be given an absolute veto over abortions.

1977

The first reported arson at an abortion clinic takes place in St. Paul, Minnesota, and the first abortion clinic bombing takes place in Cincinnati, Ohio.

1979

In *Colautti v. Franklin* the Supreme Court gives doctors broad discretion in determining fetal viability, saying the determination is up to doctors, not courts or legislatures.

1987

On November 28 Randall Terry, founder of Operation Rescue, stages his first blockade of an abortion clinic with the intent of disrupting services.

1989

In *Webster v. Reproductive Health Services* the Supreme Court provides states with new authority to limit abortion rights but stops short of reversing its 1973 decision legalizing abortion.

1992

The Supreme Court's *Planned Parenthood v. Casey* decision upholds the core of *Roe v. Wade*, prohibiting states from outlawing most abortions but allowing them to establish some restrictions.

1993

David Gunn, an abortion provider, is shot and killed in Florida.

1994

Abortion provider John Britton and his volunteer escort, James Barrett, are murdered in Florida.

1994

Congress passes the Freedom of Access to Clinics' Entrance Act, which imposes criminal penalties for conduct intended to interfere with people seeking to obtain or provide reproductive health services.

1994

Shannon Lowney and Leanne Nichols, employees at two Brookline, Massachusetts, abortion clinics, are shot and killed.

1998

A bomb at an abortion clinic in Birmingham, Alabama, kills an off-duty police officer working as a security guard, and critically injures a clinic nurse.

1998

Abortion provider Barnett Slepian is shot and killed by a sniper shooting through a window of Slepian's home.

2000

The Food and Drug Administration approves the use of mifepristone (RU-486) for medical abortion.

2000

In *Stenberg v. Carhart* the Supreme Court votes to strike down Nebraska's partial-birth abortion law because it imposed an undue restriction on women's right to abortion.

2003

President George W. Bush signs the Partial Birth Abortion Ban Act, which is nearly identical to Nebraska's law.

2004

Federal district court judges in three separate cases declare the Partial Birth Abortion Ban Act of 2003 unconstitutional.

Organizations to Contact

The Abortion Access Project
552 Massachusetts Ave., Suite 215
  Cambridge, MA 02139
(617) 661-1161 • fax: (617) 492-1915
e-mail: info@abortionaccess.org
Web site: www.abortionaccess.org

The Abortion Access Project is an organization of reproductive rights activists and women's health care providers who strive to increase accessible abortion services, improve the education of students in the health professions, and educate the public to see abortion as part of comprehensive reproductive health care.

American Civil Liberties Union (ACLU)
125 Broad St., Eighteenth Floor
  New York, NY 10004
(212) 549-2585
Web site: www.aclu.org

The American Civil Liberties Union is a national organization that works to defend Americans' civil rights guaranteed in the U.S. Constitution. The ACLU's Reproductive Freedom Project works to ensure that decisions regarding abortion are free from government interference. Volunteers help with efforts to lobby Congress and organize events to promote reproductive freedom.

Catholics for a Free Choice (CFFC)
1436 U St. NW, Suite 301
  Washington, DC 20009-3997
(202) 986-6093 • fax: (202) 332-7995
e-mail: cffc@catholicsforchoice.org
Web site: www.catholicsforchoice.org

Catholics for a Free Choice supports the right to a legal abortion. It promotes family planning to reduce the incidence of abortion and to increase women's choices in childbearing and child rearing. CFFC's Web site lists full-text articles such as "The Roman Catholic Church and Reproductive Choice" as well as summaries of pro-choice Catholic books. In addition, CFFC publishes the quarterly *Conscience* magazine.

Center for Reproductive Rights
120 Wall St., New York, NY 10005
(917) 637-3600 • fax: (917) 637-3666
e-mail: info@reprorights.org
Web site: www.crlp.org

The Center for Reproductive Rights is committed to ensuring reproductive freedom as a fundamental right through the legislature and the courts. The group's attorneys and activists focus on policy analysis, public education, and legal work. Fact sheets and briefing papers are available on the organization's Web site.

Choice USA
1010 Wisconsin Ave. NW, Suite 410
  Washington, DC 20007
(888) 784-4494 • fax: (202) 965-7701
e-mail: info@choiceusa.org
Web site: www.choiceusa.org

Choice USA provides support to the next generation of leaders who advocate reproductive choice. The group gives emerging leaders the education and tools necessary for organizing and promoting a youth-centered, pro-choice agenda. Choice USA publishes a twice-monthly newsletter that is distributed by e-mail.

Feminists for Life of America (FFLA)
PO Box 20685, Alexandria, VA 22320
(703) 836-3354
e-mail: info@feministsforlife.org
Web site: www.feministsforlife.org

FFLA is a grassroots, nonsectarian organization that works to achieve equality for women. It opposes abortion and infanticide, considering these acts inconsistent with the feminist principles of justice, nonviolence, and nondiscrimination. It publishes the quarterly journal *American Feminist.*

Human Life International
4 Family Life, Front Royal, VA 22630
(540) 635-7884 • fax: (540) 622-6247
e-mail: hli@hli.org
Web site: www.hli.org

Through prayer, service, and education, Human Life International supports the sanctity of life and family according to the teachings of the Roman Catholic Church. The organization publishes *Special Report,* a monthly newsletter covering international news and events.

Life Issues Institute
1821 W. Galbraith Rd., Cincinnati, OH 45239
(513) 729-3600
e-mail: info@lifeissues.org
Web site: www.lifeissues.org

Through its nationwide educational program, the Life Issues Institute seeks equal protection under the law for all human beings, from conception until natural death. It produces educational materials, newsletters, and radio broadcasts.

NARAL Pro-Choice America
1156 Fifteenth St. NW, Suite 700
  Washington, DC 20005
(202) 973-3000 • fax: (202) 973-3096
Web site: www.prochoiceamerica.org

The political and grassroots arm of the pro-choice movement, NARAL works to protect a woman's right to abortion. The organization's goals include reducing unwanted pregnancies, providing better access to contraception, and providing better access to reproductive information and services. NARAL publishes the quarterly *NARAL News.*

National Abortion Federation (NAF)

1755 Massachusetts Ave. NW, Suite 600
Washington, DC 20036
(202) 667-5881 • fax: (202) 667-5890
e-mail: naf@prochoice.org
Web site: www.prochoice.org

NAF is a professional association of abortion providers in the United States and Canada. It offers training and services to abortion providers. It also provides information and referral services to women. Its educational tools include CD-ROMs; patient education guides; an internationally recognized textbook, *A Clinician's Guide to Medical and Surgical Abortion*; curricular resources; fact sheets; and videos.

National Network of Abortion Funds

42 Seaverns Ave., Boston, MA 02130
(617) 524-6040 • fax: (617) 524-6042
e-mail: info@nnaf.org
Web site: www.nnaf.org

The National Network of Abortion Funds was formed to help women overcome financial barriers to securing an abortion. It publishes *Building an Abortion Fund: An Organizing Guide* as well as a video documentary titled *Legal but Out of Reach: Six Women's Abortion Stories*.

National Organization for Women

1100 H St. NW, Third Floor
Washington, DC 20005
(202) 628-8669 • fax: (202) 785-8576
e-mail: now@now.org
Web site: www.now.org

Asserting that reproductive rights are more than just matters of choice, NOW supports access to safe and legal abortion for all women. The organization opposes legislative attempts to restrict reproductive rights.

National Pro-Life Alliance
4521 Windsor Arms Ct.
  Annandale, VA 22003
(703) 321-9100
Web site: www.prolifealliance.org

The National Pro-Life Alliance works exclusively to advance legislation restricting abortion, with the ultimate goal of overturning the Supreme Court's *Roe v. Wade* decision, which legalized abortion. Members of the organization have formed a grassroots lobbying program to influence Congress on abortion-related legislation. The organization publishes the quarterly newsletter *LifeLine.*

National Right to Life Committee (NRLC)
512 Tenth St. NW, Washington, DC 20004
(202) 626-8800
e-mail: nrlc@nrlc.org
Web site: www.nrlc.org

The NRLC, a pro-life organization, was founded in response to the legalization of abortion in 1973. The organization publishes a monthly newspaper, *National Right to Life News,* and works to achieve legislative reform. Its goal is to restore legal protection to unborn children.

Planned Parenthood Federation of America
434 W. Thirty-third St.
  New York, NY 10001
(212) 541-7800 • fax: (212) 245-1845
e-mail: communications@ppfa.org
Web site: www.plannedparenthood.org

Planned Parenthood advocates the right of every person to decide when and whether to have a child. The organization provides information and services related to reproductive decisions, including contraception and abortion, and publishes an online newsletter, *Choice!*

Pro-Life Action League
6160 N. Cicero Ave., Chicago, IL 60646

(773) 777-2900 • fax: (773) 777-3061
e-mail: info@prolifeaction.org
Web site: www.prolifeaction.org

Founded in 1980, the Pro-Life Action League attempts to save unborn children through nonviolent direct action. Its methods include maintaining a presence at abortion clinics, public protests, confronting abortion providers, broadcasting the pro-life message, and youth outreach. It publishes an online magazine, *Pro-Life Action News*.

Religious Coalition for Reproductive Choice
1025 Vermont Ave. NW, Suite 1130
   Washington, DC 20005
(202) 628-7700 • fax: (202) 628-7716
e-mail: info@rcrc.org
Web site: www.rcrc.org

Established in 1973 by both clergy and laity, the Religious Coalition for Reproductive Choice is an alliance of national organizations from major faiths that are committed to preserving reproductive choice as a basic part of religious liberty. The organization supports abortion rights, opposes antiabortion violence, and educates policy makers and the public about the diversity of religious perspectives on abortion. Among the coalition's publications is the Speak Out! series.

For Further Reading

Books

Patricia Baird-Windle and Eleanor J. Bader, *Targets of Hatred: Anti-Abortion Terrorism*. New York: Palgrave, 2001.

Dallas A. Blanchard and Terry J. Prewitt, *Religious Violence and Abortion: The Gideon Project*. Gainesville: University Press of Florida, 1993.

Janet Farrell Brodie, *Contraception and Abortion in Nineteenth-Century America*. Ithaca, NY: Cornell University Press, 1994.

Guy Condon and David Hazard, *Fatherhood Aborted*. Wheaton, IL: Tyndale House, 2001.

Marian Faux, *Roe v. Wade: The Untold Story of the Landmark Supreme Court Decision That Made Abortion Legal*. New York: Cooper Square, 2001.

Norman F. Ford, *When Did I Begin? Conception of the Human Individual in History, Philosophy and Science*. Cambridge, UK: Cambridge University Press, 1988.

Faye Ginsburg, *Contested Lives*. Berkeley: University of California Press, 1989.

Cynthia Gorney, *Articles of Faith: A Frontline History of the Abortion Wars*. New York: Simon & Schuster, 1998.

Mark Youngblood Herring, *The Pro-Life/Choice Debate*. Westport, CT: Greenwood, 2003.

Lawrence M. Hinman, *Contemporary Moral Issues: Diversity and Consensus*. Upper Saddle River, NJ: Pearson Prentice-Hall, 2005.

Jane Hurst, *The History of Abortion in the Catholic Church: The Untold Story*. Washington, DC: Catholics for a Free Choice, 1989.

Ted G. Jelen, ed., *Perspectives on the Politics of Abortion.* Westport, CT: Praeger, 1995.

Felicia Lowenstein, *The Abortion Battle: Looking at Both Sides.* Springfield, NJ: Enslow, 1996.

Carol J.C. Maxwell, *Pro-Life Activists in America: Meaning, Motivation, and Direct Action.* New York: Cambridge University Press, 2002.

Norma McCorvey with Andy Meisler, *I Am Roe.* New York: HarperCollins, 1994.

Norma McCorvey with Gary Thomas, *Won by Love.* Nashville, TN: T. Nelson, 1997.

Patricia G. Miller, *The Worst of Times.* New York: HarperCollins, 1993.

Harold J. Morowitz and James S. Trefil, *The Facts of Life: Science and the Abortion Controversy.* New York: Oxford University Press, 1992.

Marvin Olasky, *Abortion Rites: A Social History of Abortion in America.* Washington, DC: Regnery, 1995.

John M. Riddle, *Eve's Herbs: A History of Contraception and Abortion in the West.* Cambridge, MA: Harvard University Press, 1997.

Carl Sagan and Ann Druyan, *Billions and Billions.* New York: Ballantine, 1997.

Alexander Sanger, *Beyond Choice: Reproductive Freedom in the 21st Century.* New York: PublicAffairs, 2004.

Ricki Solinger, ed., *Abortion Wars: A Half Century of Struggle, 1950–2000.* Berkeley: University of California Press, 1998.

Suzanne Staggenborg, *The Pro-Choice Movement: Organization and Activism in the Abortion Conflict.* New York: Oxford University Press, 1991.

Teresa R. Wagner, ed., *Back to the Drawing Board: The Future of the Pro-Life Movement.* South Bend, IN: St. Augustine's, 2003.

Faye Wattleton, *Life on the Line.* New York: Ballantine, 1996.

Periodicals

Anita Allen, "Drug Counter Is No Place for Political Protest," *Sunday Patriot-News*, May 15, 2005.

Dick Bohrer, "Deception-on-Demand," *Moody Monthly*, May 1980.

Jodi Enda, "The Women's View," *American Prospect*, April 2005.

Lawrence B. Finer et al., "Reasons U.S. Women Have Abortions: Quantitative and Qualitative Perspectives," *Perspectives on Sexual and Reproductive Health*, September 2005.

Carl Golden, "Voice of Reason Against Far-Right Ideology," *Bergen Record*, August 2, 2005.

Linn Duvall Harwell, "Repeal of Comstock Law Provided Us Reproductive Rights," *Post-Tribune*, June 8, 2005.

Michael A. Lipton, "Agony of Choice," *People Weekly*, June 22, 1992.

Kathryn Jean Lopez, "Women Deserve Better," *Human Life Review*, Winter 2003.

Anna Quindlen, "Now Available: Middle Ground," *Newsweek*, July 11, 2005.

William Raspberry, "Fine Line Between Partial-Birth Abortion, Infanticide," *State Journal Register*, July 17, 1998.

Cathy Cleaver Ruse, "Partial-Birth Abortion on Trial," *Human Life Review*, Spring 2005.

Peter Schrag, "Parental Consent: The Sleeper in the Abortion Fight," *Sacramento Bee*, July 6, 2005.

Peter Slevin, "Stem Cell Research Meets Fierce Opposition," *Washington Post*, August 10, 2005.

Internet Sources

Harry Blackmun and William Rehnquist, *Roe v. Wade*, Case #410US113. http://caselaw.lp.findlaw.com/scripts/getcase.pl?court=US&vol=410&invol=113.

CNN.com, "Poll: Americans Back Abortion Limits, Oppose Ban," November 27, 2005. www.cnn.com/2005/US/11/27/abortion.poll.

Cynthia Dailard, "Abortion in Context: United States and Worldwide," Guttmacher Institute, May 1999. www.agi-usa.org/pubs/ib_0599.html.

Scott F. Gilbert and Emily Zackin, "When Does Human Life Begin?" Bioethics for Developmental Biologists, April 17, 2003. www.devbio.com/article.php?id=162.

Stanley K. Henshaw and Dina J. Feivelson, "Teenage Abortion and Pregnancy Statistics by State, 1996," Guttmacher Institute, November/December 2000. www.agi-usa.org/pubs/journals/3227200.html.

Stacey Kalish, "Lingering Thoughts About Abortion: Male Grief Is Hidden," *Psychology Today*, May/June 2004. www.findarticles.com/p/articles/mi_m1175/is_3_37/ai_n6097586.

John F. Kavanaugh, "Abortion, Faith and Politics," *America*, February 16, 2004. www.americamagazine.org/gettext.cfm?articleTypeID=7&textID=3412&issueID=472.

Alex Markels, "Supreme Court's Evolving Rulings on Abortion," NPR.org, November 30, 2005. www.npr.org/templates/story/story.php?storyId=5029934.

ReligiousTolerance.org, "Stem Cell Research: All Sides to the Dispute." www.religioustolerance.org/res_stem.htm.

Index